Raising
Raffi

Raising Raffi

The First Five Years

Keith Gessen

VIKING

VIKING
An imprint of Penguin Random House LLC
penguinrandomhouse.com

The following essays were published previously in different form and some under
different titles: "Home Birth" as "I Had No Idea What Fatherhood Was Going to Be
Like" (*The Cut*), "Say It in Russian" as "Why Did I Teach My Son to Speak Russian?"
(*The New Yorker*), "Love and Anger" (*The New Yorker*), "A School for Raffi" as
"School Daze" (*n+1*), "King Germ" as "What Is Distance Learning For?" (*The New
Yorker*), and "Game Time" (*The New York Times Magazine*).

Grateful acknowledgment is made for permission to reprint the following:

Translation of "This Is How Hunger Begins" by Daniil Kharms. Translated by Robert
Chandler. Used with permission of the translator.

"A Man Once Walked Out of His House," by Daniil Kharms from *Oberiu: An
Anthology of Russian Absurdism*, translated by Matvei Yankelevich and Eugene
Ostashevsky. Evanston: Northwestern University Press, 2006, p. 140. Copyright © 2006
by Northwestern University Press. Published 2006. Used with permission of
Northwestern University Press. All rights reserved.

ISBN 9780593300442 (hardcover)
ISBN 9780593300459 (ebook)

Printed in the United States of America
1st Printing

Set in Stempel Garamond LT Pro
Designed by Cassandra Garruzzo Mueller

For Emily

Contents

Raising Raffi

Author's Note

I wrote this book out of desperation.

For the first few months of my son Raffi's life, I felt like I was merely surviving. Through the sleeplessness and terror, I put one parenting foot in front of the other and tried not to look too far ahead. But when this passed, what I wanted, more than anything, was to talk. I had never before experienced such a contradictory mass of feelings; had never engaged in an activity so simultaneously mundane and significant; had never met anyone like screaming two-month-old Raffi, or cuddly one-year-old Raffi ("Uck," he would say, when he wanted a hug), or scourge of our household two-and-a-half-year-old Raffi. Through each of these phases I was amazed by his transformations, his progress, and my own complicated reactions. I wanted to know if other people were going through the same.

Parents talked, of course. My wife, the writer Emily Gould, and I talked all the time about Raffi, and we sought out other parents on the playgrounds, on street corners, even on the subway. Some of us, when we talked, couldn't help but brag. "He started sleeping through the night last week," someone might say, alienating their interlocutor forever. Or: "His grandparents took him for the weekend, and we slept late." (An active in-town grandparent was worth, by my informal calculations, about forty thousand dollars a year.) Others went in the other direction. Their child wouldn't nap; he threw his food onto the floor; he bit a kid in day care. Emily and I were in the self-deprecating camp. But of course this left out something, too—the physical joy of being with Raffi, the hilarity of much of what he did. There was, in short, a limit to what you could get at when chatting with other parents. I felt like these conversations never went far enough.

There were books about parenting. Some of them were very good; most were not. In its main current, parenting literature was the literature of advice. The books diagnosed a sickness— your child's sleep "problem," your son's behavior "issue"—and promised to solve it. When the solution didn't work, you blamed yourself. Then you sought out another book, one that would "work" better, and went through the cycle again.

There was a particular gap, I thought, in the dad literature. In the few books out there, we were either stupid dad, who can't do anything right, or superdad, a self-proclaimed feminist and caretaker. I was sure those dads existed, but I didn't know any. The dads I knew took their parenting responsibilities seriously, were not idiots, and did their best around the house and with the kids. With some notable exceptions, they did less parenting than their spouses. (The gay dads I knew hired a lot of child care.) Nonetheless, they thought it was one of the most important things they were going to do with their lives.

At the time I started working on this book, when Raffi had just turned three, I was supposed to be doing other things. I had a novel coming out that I needed to promote, and then a nonfiction book on U.S.–Russia relations that I should have been researching. But I couldn't stop thinking about Raffi: about our situation with him; about the situation of all parents with their little kids. I began taking notes and eventually I started writing these essays.

I felt ridiculous about it at times. To write about parenting when you are a father is like writing about literature when you can hardly read. Almost without exception, in every male-female relationship I encountered, the mothers knew more about their kids than the fathers and parented them better. My own relationship was no exception. Emily was an extremely well-informed parent who also, not long after Raffi was born, started writing occasional essays about him. I love those essays as much as anything she has written. But there were things that I did with Raffi—talk Russian, play sports, *yell* in Russian—that were particular to my experience. And I came to think there was some value in recording my own groping toward knowledge in this most important of human endeavors, a kind of record of a primitive consciousness making its way toward the light. I was part of the first generation of men who, for various reasons, were spending more time with their kids than previous generations. That seemed notable to me.

I recently asked my own father if he remembered my second-grade teacher, Ms. Lynch, because I had just called her up to interview her about education. He said he didn't, and wouldn't. "But you must have gone to the parent-teacher conferences?" I said. "Oh no," said my dad. "I was at work." My father had relocated us halfway around the world so that we wouldn't have to grow up in the Soviet Union; drove me to every single hockey game I ever played in from the ages of six to sixteen, which was hundreds of hockey games; almost never traveled for work; and taught me math, physics, how to drive, and how to throw a left hook. He was hardly an absent father. But to him the idea of attending a parent-teacher conference was risible, whereas I consider the quarterly parent-teacher conferences for Raffi major events in my life.

This book consists of nine essays, arranged by subject: birth, zero to two, bilingualism, discipline, picture books, schools, the pandemic, sports, and cross-cultural parenting. Each of the essays describes my experience as a parent; draws on some of the literature and conversations I've found most helpful (or unhelpful) in thinking through this experience; and comes or doesn't come to a conclusion. I've tried to make it so that the essays can be read independently, if a busy parent doesn't have any interest in, for example, bilingualism; but I've also sought to avoid repetition and placed things in a more or less chronological way so that a reader going through the entire book can see Raffi (and me and his mother) slowly moving into the future.

Most of the material is from my personal experience, though

as you'll see, one of the things I do to understand my experience is read. Where appropriate, I have also used my training as a journalist to talk with some of the people I thought would have the most to say on a given subject, whether it's the purpose of education, the nature of Russian parenting, or the lessons of parenting research in comparative perspective. I hope these conversations do not seem out of place; they were important to me in thinking through these issues.

I wrote some of these essays earlier than others, and in instances where I have changed my mind or learned a lot more about the subject—for example, by having another child and seeing him, at age three, suddenly turn from angel to avenger—I have tried to incorporate that later insight into the text. The thing I've learned about parenting, the thing that the parenting books don't tell you, is that *time* is the only solution. You do eventually figure it out, or start to. But by then it is often too late. The damage—to your child, yourself, your marriage—has already been done. That is the way of knowledge, though. In its purest form, it always comes too late.

Home Birth

I was not prepared to be a father—this much I knew. I didn't have a job and I lived in one of the most expensive cities on the planet. I had always assumed that I'd have kids, but I had spent zero minutes thinking about them. In short, though not young, I was stupid.

Emily told me she was pregnant when we were walking down Thirty-Fourth Street in Manhattan, on the way to Macy's to shop for wedding rings. Our wedding was a few weeks away, and I had, as usual, put off preparing until the last minute. I had a fellowship at the time at the New York Public Library in midtown, and I must have googled "wedding rings near me." Macy's it was. All around us on Thirty-Fourth Street people were shopping and hurrying and driving and honking. Emily told me, and I thought, "OK. Here we go. We are going to have a kid."

Then I thought: We need to get some very cheap wedding rings at Macy's.

I WAS BORN IN MOSCOW and came to the United States with my parents and older sibling when I was six. I grew up in a suburb outside of Boston and found it boring and dreamed of leaving to become a writer. After college, I moved to New York and worked odd jobs and wrote short stories, which I sent to literary magazines, which never wrote me back. To see my name in print, I started doing journalism. I found I really liked it. I also started translating things—stories, an oral history, poems—from Russian. Traveling to Russia and seeing its version of capitalism up close converted me to democratic socialism. Eventually I started a left-wing literary magazine, *n+1*, with some friends, published a novel, and traveled as much as possible to Russia to write about it. This was a decent literary career, truly more than I ever could have hoped for, but it did not bring in a lot of income; when Emily and I met I was living with two roommates in a grand but ancient and cockroach-infested apartment on Eastern Parkway in Brooklyn.

At the time, Emily was a writer for *Gawker*, a media gossip website. She was brilliant, beautiful, and very funny; she could also be very mean. She had grown up in an upper-middle-class household in suburban Maryland, but she had a chip on her shoulder. She was also a very good cook. We dated for a while, broke up (she dumped me at a Starbucks in Cobble Hill that later closed during the pandemic), and then started dating again. Eventually we moved in together, to an apartment above a bar in Bedford-Stuyvesant. By this point Emily had quit working for *Gawker* and published a well-received book of essays. With her best friend, Ruth, she started a small feminist publishing house, Emily Books; she worked for a while at a publishing start-up, then got sick of it. The year she got pregnant, she published her first novel, *Friendship*, about two best friends whose relationship is disrupted when one of them gets . . . pregnant. I was working on my second novel, about Russia, and had received a yearlong fellowship at the New York Public Library to research and write it. The fellowship was the bulk of our income that year. Strictly speaking, we still didn't have much money, but that was OK, because we also didn't have any kids.

Now, at Macy's, we couldn't get the attention of the saleswoman in the giant ring section. I would have hung around until she got to us, but Emily looked disappointed—the mother of my child! I couldn't make her wait. We got on the subway to Brooklyn and bought rings above our budget at a cute little store in Williamsburg.

I suppose it isn't exactly true that I hadn't thought about kids. I hadn't thought about actual birth, or what sort of clothes a baby wears, or about the practicalities of early infancy. "As a child, from the moment I gained some understanding of what it entailed, I worried about childbirth," writes Rachel Cusk in *A Life's Work*, her dark, brilliant memoir of motherhood. She feared its pain and its violence and what would happen on the other side. To this, truly, I had given zero thought.

But I see in retrospect that I had spent years steeling myself for the eventuality of a "family." I had imbibed the heroic male literature of family neglect: Henry James, who skipped a family funeral because he was finishing a story ("One has no business to have any children," one of his characters famously says. "I mean of course if one wants to do anything good"); Philip Roth, who refused to have children; Tolstoy, who had many children and a long marriage but who still managed, at the very end of his life, to walk out on them. F. Scott Fitzgerald wrote beautiful letters on life and literature to his daughter, Frances, but only after Zelda had been committed to a mental institution and Fitzgerald himself was floundering in Hollywood. "The intellect of man must choose," William Butler Yeats had written: "Perfection of the life, or of the work." I would choose the work, I told myself over and over. I had been married once before, while still in college, and at the time I was adamant that the relationship must not interfere with my writing. My time must be my own; I must have adequate amounts of it; if my writing does not get done, then all is lost. My insistence on this eventually doomed the relationship. We broke up. The lesson I took from this was not that I should keep things in perspective, but that I should arrange my life so it revolved wholly around literature. In the pages of *n+1* I pledged never to teach writing, or to write for money, or to do anything else to distract from what I thought of as the highest calling one could have.

One time, not long after Emily and I had started dating, I hosted the Russian writer Ludmilla Petrushevskaya in New York. With Anya, my ex-wife, I had translated a book of her scary fairy tales, and Petrushevskaya, by then in her seventies, flew over to do some readings, shop for clothes for her kids at Century 21, and eat Thai food. She was, and is, in my opinion, the greatest living Russian writer, the final chronicler of that country's life at the end of its most terrible century. One evening toward the end of her stay, while we were eating Thai food, she suddenly looked at me and said, apropos of nothing, "You know, Kostya, I started writing when I was a little girl. But I didn't become a real writer until I had my first child." I don't know why she decided to say this to me. Maybe she was just talking. But at the time I thought it was because she saw in me a person leading a superfluous existence, a too-easy life. I had thought I'd made my life pure so I could devote it to literature. That's not what Petrushevskaya saw.

Now here I was, five years later. I was going to be a father. I was elated, and I was scared. This was serious business, involving doctors, nurses, life and death. Immediately I was worried about the baby. Was he comfortable? Was he safe? Was he getting the proper nutrients? At the same time, I started trying to figure out, almost despite myself, how I was going to make sure the baby didn't interfere with my work. I had a vague foreboding that he would, though I couldn't quite figure out why. What *exactly* was so time-consuming about parenthood? Why couldn't people sleep? And work? When a baby was little, couldn't you rock his cradle as you answered emails or wrote a novel? When a baby was crying at night, couldn't you put in earplugs? I was worried about the baby, but worried, too, about myself.

I had one friend from graduate school, Eric, with whom I'd kept in touch after the birth of his child. I asked him out for a beer and told him that Emily was pregnant. I asked, "What do I need to know?"

"It's tough," Eric said. "It's not easy. You need a lot of stuff."

Stuff?

"Yeah, a lot of stuff."

Stuff. Of course! What we needed was stuff! I was delighted. Stuff was something I could handle. Emily and I started getting stuff. I bought a kid's dresser—with a little nook up top for a changing pad—from some Russians in Sheepshead Bay. Emily's friend Jess gave us her daughter's old crib. Emily's friend Lori gave us a bassinet. Eric, who planned to have another kid, loaned us a second bassinet. Emily's parents bought us a car seat and a stroller. My father bought us the mattress for the crib. My friend A. J., who'd just had a baby, mailed us what looked like a large pillow with a little depression in it, which she called a "dog bed," for putting our future baby down onto. We bought some onesies and some diapers and a changing pad. One day Eric's wife, Rachael, a clothing designer, came by our place with a baby carrier. Her daughter was asleep in the car downstairs. Technically, I think, this was illegal. Rachael threw the carrier onto our bed. "Here," she said. Someone had sent a stuffed bunny for the future baby and Rachael grabbed him by the throat and put him in the carrier. She secured one strap around her waist, then bent down over the bunny and threaded her arms through the shoulder straps. "Like that," she said. We nodded, uncomprehending. "OK, bye," said Rachael, and ran back down the stairs to her daughter. We were in awe. We now had a baby carrier.

The stuff was great. It kept the fear at bay. If the baby showed up tomorrow, we'd have a place to lay him down while he slept; a surface on which to change his diapers; methods to transport him by street or car. But still we were scared.

Or maybe I should stop saying "we."

Before the baby, Emily and I were pretty similar. We both liked to drink coffee and read books and work on our laptops, sometimes together, at the café on the corner; we liked drinking a medium amount of alcohol with dinner; before going to bed we liked to watch an HBO show and eat a chocolate bar. If we were on the beach, we liked to go swimming. Emily was on her high school's swim team and remained an excellent swimmer. We liked going to the movies.

Emily becoming pregnant both brought us closer and pushed us apart. For a while, including at our wedding, we were the only ones who knew. Then, later on, we were the ones to whom every little thing mattered: at the ultrasounds, we studied the expression on the face of the lab tech; we worried about the blood tests coming back; we examined the little sonogram photos to see if we could make out the features and character of our future baby.

But there was also no denying that this was all happening to Emily, inside of Emily, and not inside of me. It was as if we'd discovered that Emily had a superpower. I worshipped her.

We were scared of different things, then, and in different ways. I was scared of my ignorance. Emily was scared of physical pain. But Emily was also prepared. She had read the literature and she knew lots of moms. Once she became pregnant, she downloaded an app to her phone that told her all about the baby. "Our baby is the size of a pea," she would tell me. Then: "Our baby is the size of a plum." Eventually our baby was the size of an eggplant. He was in good hands with Emily. The weak link was me.

TIME, AT LEAST, was on my side. Later on, time would turn on me. As I stood there swinging or rocking our baby so he would fall asleep; or walking him around the neighborhood in his stroller so he would fall asleep; or just kind of hanging out with him aimlessly, waiting for him to fall asleep, time moved too slowly. But during the pregnancy, time was my friend. Nine months was almost enough time for even me to get my act together. Through the sheer accumulation of days, I sometimes hoped, wisdom would come upon me.

Emily wanted a home birth. I thought this was crazy. Modern medicine had come so far! But she said she didn't want to take a cab to the hospital and possibly give birth in it. This made sense. I imagined looking up at the taxi meter as my child was born and seeing, like, $198. I agreed to explore the option of home birth.

On Netflix we watched an unconvincing documentary called *The Business of Being Born*, in which former daytime talk show host Ricki Lake, pregnant with her second child, sings the praises of home birth and denounces the American hospital system, which pumps women full of drugs and then forces them to have

C-sections they don't need. Toward the end of the film, Lake gives beautiful birth at home, no drugs needed. The director of the film is also pregnant, but ends up giving birth at the hospital because her baby is coming out the wrong way (legs or butt first, known as "breech," as in breeches). The film is pretty compelling as an indictment of a savage and profit-seeking medical establishment. But in proposing home birth as a sort of opt-out movement, it is much less so. There are a lot of people who cannot or should not give birth at home. When the director has to "transfer" to the hospital to get an emergency C-section, the news ought to be that her baby has survived. But in the context of the home-birthing paradigm, the director is made to seem like a failure.

Still, that didn't mean we couldn't have a home birth. We interviewed a midwife named B. She was young and seemed nice enough, but as we were wrapping up, she said a very strange thing. "I have a question for you," she said. "If something goes wrong, will you still remain advocates of home birth?"

It took us a moment to process the question. If something goes wrong? With our *baby*? Will we be what? Of *what*? "Sure," we managed, but what we were thinking was: Why would anything go wrong? And why would someone in her right mind ask that of two terrified people who had never given birth before? It felt like the midwife had an ideological commitment to home birth that went beyond her commitment to our unborn baby. It did not feel right.

I was not unwilling to discuss the possibility of something

going wrong. In fact, I very much wanted to know what would happen if something went wrong: what our backup plan was; what hospital we'd go to and what doctor we would see. But I had no interest in discussing my advocacy or nonadvocacy of home birth in that scenario.

We continued to do research and talk to people. One friend warned me that his daughter's shoulders had gotten stuck on her way out of the womb and that the doctor had reached in, deliberately broken her collarbone, and got her out. "Can't do that at home," he said. (Actually, this is not true—shoulder dystocia, as I later learned this was called, can be handled at home in the same way.) Another friend, whose husband was a doctor, said she couldn't believe people gave birth at home in bathtubs. "The baby can't breathe underwater!" she said. This also was incorrect—the baby has been breathing through the umbilical cord for months, and anyway, you were supposed to pull him out of the water immediately. But these bits of advice stuck with me and scared me. I was becoming increasingly concerned about home birth. Then we met Karen and Martine.

Karen and Martine were midwives in their fifties who ran a joint practice and had been doing this for years. Practically the first thing out of their mouths was a list of all that could go wrong with a home birth, every eventuality that would trigger the dreaded transfer to the hospital. A breech baby, like in the Ricki Lake film, to be sure, as there's no way to turn him right side up again at home. Or a baby whose heart rate isn't strong enough, indicating that he might be tangled in the umbilical cord. A baby turned the wrong way laterally rather than verti-cally, i.e., with his back to the mother's back, is tricky but not impossible to deliver at home. (You can, at least theoretically, turn the baby around through the mother's stomach with a towel.) There were several other scenarios along these lines. Karen and Martine described these before—in fact, instead of—describing how natural and wonderful a home birth was. They weren't trying to sell us on home birth. They seemed instead to be saying that if our commitment to home birth was stronger than our commitment to the health of our unborn baby, or of his mother, then they did not want to work with us.

I was so relieved and grateful. I thought it would be a great honor to have our baby delivered by Karen or Martine. Emily agreed. We decided to have the birth at home.

Karen and Martine recommended a birth class specifically devoted to home births. This, too, was a hit. Our teacher was a lovely artist named Ellen. Every Tuesday for seven weeks we would sit on cushions in her living room alongside six other couples and discuss the birth process for two hours. We learned about the events leading up to labor: Braxton-Hicks contrac-tions, which seem like contractions but aren't; pre-labor, when the contractions start becoming more regular; and the com-mencement of official labor with the rupturing of the amniotic sac (the water breaking). We learned that labor itself had three stages: early labor, active labor, and then the "transition" phase. Early labor was relatively mild; active labor was painful and prolonged, and that was when you called the midwife; once the midwife arrived, the mother started pushing to get the baby out—transitioning him from the womb to the world.

It was a great class. I had absorbed from popular culture that birth classes taught women some kind of elaborate breathing technique for their contractions, but this had gone out of style. Rather than breathing in some specific way during active labor, Ellen advised women to do what comes naturally when you are in pain: to scream.

I WAS BECOMING MORE PREPARED, but I still wasn't prepared. We bought and borrowed and accepted stuff; hired our midwives; wrote a letter to our insurance carrier asking them to pay for a home birth; took the class. We even came up with a sort of name for the baby, so we wouldn't always have to call him "the baby." It was a Russian name, in honor of my Russian heritage, but also the most implausible (to us) Russian name that we could think of—Yuri. It was implausible because, as Emily pointed out, mean kids would just call our baby Urine.

Still, it all seemed pretty unreal. Summer came. The library fellowship I was on ended. I returned all my books and cleared out my office. I was playing a lot of beer league hockey. Emily was writing an essay. We went about our lives.

Two weeks from the due date, with our baby now the size of a small watermelon, we had an appointment with Karen. For the first seven months of the pregnancy, we (or most often, just

Emily) had to travel to various offices, whether Karen's or Martine's, or to the labs or medical offices where they had technology that Karen and Martine did not: Emily got ultrasounds in midtown and a blood test in Bay Ridge. Everything was fine. Our baby was a boy and had no genetic deformities. In the last two months, and this was a true luxury of home birth, the midwives came to our apartment. One reason was that it gave them a sense of our place for the day of the birth. But it was also a courtesy to the mother, to Emily, who by this point found it unpleasant to travel.

On this day, Karen went through her usual routine. She asked Emily how she was feeling, asked after her diet, and measured her stomach. All was in order. Then she took out a little heart rate kit, spread some oil on Emily's stomach, and listened for the baby's heartbeat.

We all heard it: thump-thump-thump-thump-silence. The fifth beat was missing. Thump-thump-thump-thump-silence. We looked at Karen, hoping she would say it was nothing, but she seemed concerned. Thump-thump-thump-thump-silence. She turned off the machine and turned it back on again. Thump-thump-thump-thump-silence.

"You need to go see a pediatric cardiologist," she said.

I imagined making an appointment, waiting for the baby to be born, then figuring out a way to transport him to the doctor.

"Now," said Karen. "Today."

While we sat there in shock, Karen got on the phone and

called a practice she knew in Union Square. She asked if they took our insurance. They did. Karen said we'd be coming right in.

I looked it up on Google Maps, which said that a cab and the subway would both take half an hour. But in my experience Google consistently underestimates traffic wait times. I imagined us sitting in traffic on Fourteenth Street with our little baby and his missing heartbeat. "I think we should take the train," I said. Emily shrugged. She didn't care. Karen drove us the three blocks to the subway and told us to call her after the appointment. She let us out, and then we were on our own.

It took a while for the G train to come. The platform, like most New York City subway platforms during the summer, was filthy. There was trash on the tracks, with rats scurrying this way and that, arranging their housekeeping. Some kind of water leaked slowly from a pipe near the ceiling. Emily looked really pregnant now, and I felt useless and lost. The baby, visible in Emily's stomach, was nonetheless for me a total abstraction. Almost nothing in my life had actually changed. I had bought the dresser, put together the crib, attended the birth classes, and then basically checked out. Was I being punished in some way? Was there something I should have noticed, something that I'd missed, because I wasn't paying enough attention?

To lighten the mood, I started saying something about Yuri. "THAT'S NOT HIS NAME!" Emily said.

I stopped whatever it was that I was saying.

And Yuri was, indeed, not to be his name.

Forty minutes later, at the cardiologist's office, a poker-faced young woman took a number of photos of our baby's little heart. Then the cardiologist came in and told us not to worry. There were two kinds of prenatal heart conditions that this could have been, and our baby had the benign version. Lots of stuff goes haywire in the brief period when the baby is preparing to leave the womb and enter the world, said the cardiologist. The entire respiratory apparatus has to reorganize itself to take in oxygen from the air instead of the umbilical cord. Sometimes there are hitches. Most of the time, they get worked out in the process of birth. He said to come see him once the baby was born, but for the moment he thought we were OK.

SIX DAYS LATER, I came home from a hockey game at midnight. Emily was up, watching a show in what was still the TV room, though the children's dresser and crib were already hinting that its time was running out. "My contractions have started," she said. But her water hadn't broken. These could be Braxton-Hicks contractions or the actual contractions of pre-labor. Emily thought they were the real thing. Luckily, Martine was coming the next morning for the final pre-birth checkup. We went to sleep.

In the morning, Martine was happy to hear about the contractions. She checked the baby's heartbeat. Thump-thump-thump-thump-silence. As Martine was doing the rest of the checkup, a large black spot appeared on Emily's sweatpants.

"Uh," she said.

"Ah," said Martine.

It was her water breaking: official labor had commenced! Martine, as always, was very calm. "Call me when the contractions are stronger and more frequent," she said—and left! She had other stuff to do. We were a little bit surprised. It was eleven A.M.

For the next four hours, we hung out, watched a bunch of TV, and waited. "The one thing you must not do," my friend George had told me, "is buy a bag of Milano cookies and eat them all while Emily is giving birth." Apparently George, waiting in the hospital before the most active phase of his wife's labor started, had become a little peckish and gone out to a deli and bought some Milanos. Then while she gave birth, he sort of stood there and mindlessly ate them all. They really are very delicious. Four years later she still had not forgiven him.

I managed not to eat a bunch of cookies, but I did make a mistake; we were watching a TV show that I thought was very funny, and I was delightedly laughing at it and so was Emily. But I failed to notice the moment she stopped laughing. She had been sitting next to me on a yoga blanket, occasionally getting on all fours during a contraction, but now her contractions had increased in magnitude. "What are you doing?!" Emily said as I laughed at our show. She was on all fours again, but grimacing. I turned off the TV.

I was the timekeeper and in a way the gatekeeper for the eventual call to Martine, and I was convinced that I would fuck it up by calling her too early. She would show up, say I was exaggerating the severity of the contractions, and leave. Then, after she left, Emily would give birth. It would be a catastrophe. But the contractions were very clear. They started getting closer and closer together and lasting longer too. The formula was 5-1-1: the contractions were to be less than five minutes apart, and last for longer than one minute, for one hour. I couldn't really understand how a contraction could last longer than a minute, but then I saw Emily visibly in pain, moaning, groaning, wincing, for an entire minute, and was convinced. At four P.M., I called the doula Emily had hired and told her she should come. Then I read to her from the piece of paper on which I was recording the contraction statistics. "Should I call the midwife?" I asked.

"Yes!" she said. I called Martine.

She and her assistant came two hours later. By then the contractions were even stronger and more frequent. Emily threw up. She was in unbelievable pain, and the hard part was still to come. She started pushing at around seven. She pushed in our living room, then on the floor of our bedroom, and finally on our bed. Throughout the period of active labor, Martine's assistant kept checking the baby's heartbeat. Thump-thump-thump-thump-silence. Thump-thump-thump-thump-silence. But Emily kept pushing, and screaming, and pushing. There was a lot of blood. Some people say that gravity is your friend when you are getting the baby out, but there's also something to be said for lying down and being maximally comfortable. Gravity, on its own, is not strong enough to get that baby out of you. At one point, when Emily was on the bed, just before the baby's head started coming out, a geyser of blood shot out from her vagina. On the advice of our midwives, we had placed a plastic shower curtain under our bedding, so that blood wouldn't get on the mattress, but the bloody geyser was not something we'd anticipated. It was high enough and strong enough that it got on our window shades. I made a mental note to get some new ones at Home Depot.

And then, about half an hour later, the baby was out! There was a terrifying moment when he didn't say anything. It was a very short moment, because right after that he started screaming. He was fine; the baby was fine. Emily and I looked at each other and laughed. We were so happy and relieved. We couldn't believe we had managed to do it—that Emily had managed to do it. At home; in our bed from IKEA; in our apartment above a bar. The assistant listened to the baby's heartbeat again: thump-thump-thump-thump-thump. Thump-thump-thump-thump-thump. Just like that, the missing beat was gone. Thump-thump-thump-thump-thump.

Martine cut the umbilical cord with a pair of surgical scissors and then let me weigh the baby on a little portable scale. Seven pounds, four ounces. Martine filled out some paperwork. Our very helpful doula helped Emily figure out how to place the baby on her breast so that he would be comfortable eating.

We decided to call him Raphael—after my grandmother Ruzya, who had died just a few months earlier; and after Emily's beloved cat Raffles, who had also recently died; and because, in Hebrew, Raphael was *rafa* (healed) and *-el* (God)—"healed by God." He had been healed of his heart condition in the moment of his birth. For a while we argued over whether "Raffi" or "Raphy" was the proper spelling of his diminutive—Emily thought Raffi, I thought Raphy—but eventually I gave in. Raffi it was.

While we lay in the bedroom with Raffi, who looked like a little gremlin, Martine and her assistant and the doula cleaned up all the blood and gore and other stuff that had gotten messed up in all the excitement. And then they left. Emily had given birth at 11:18 P.M., and by 3:00 A.M. they were gone. Our apartment was clean and empty. It was a Tuesday night; the whole neighborhood was asleep. But we were not asleep. They had left us with a little baby, and we had no idea what to do.

Zero to Two (The Age of Advice)

Suddenly there was so much advice: from our parents, from our friends, from strangers, and then of course from books and the internet. It was all moving in a hundred different directions, and the places where one picked up actually meaningful advice seemed random. Several of my male friends with children, when I talked to them about it beforehand, toed the party line. "It's awful," they said. "It's hell." But one afternoon in Manhattan a few months before Raffi was born, I happened to run into a guy I knew named Jeff. His wife had just given birth to their first child. On Sixth Avenue, in Chelsea, Jeff looked crazed, sleep-deprived, manic. I congratulated him and said that Emily, too, was pregnant. He grabbed my elbow and looked with his bloodshot eyes into mine. "It's incredible," he said. "It's the greatest thing." He seemed truly insane for a second, and then he was off, in search of something for his baby. And who was right, then: the guys who said it was hell, or half-crazed Jeff, who said it was the greatest thing? I didn't know. I still don't know.

Very quickly after Raffi was born I learned the answers to

some of my earlier questions. There turned out to be two reasons you can't sleep when your baby is little. The first is that a baby is always waking up to eat: his stomach is too little to fit more than a few hours' worth of food. So even though a baby sleeps, cumulatively, a fair amount—as much as sixteen hours a day, at first—the longest continuous stretch he's asleep is more like two hours. You are constantly being woken up. But even when the baby is quietly sleeping, you still cannot sleep, because you are worried that the baby is going to die. It is not a rational fear—statistically speaking very few babies actually die—but the fact is that some do. The phenomenon has a terrifying name—sudden infant death syndrome, SIDS—and, though very rare, it happens. A couple that lived in Brooklyn and worked, like us, in publishing had lost their three-month-old baby to SIDS when Raffi was one month old. They dropped him off for his first day of day care and he died there during his nap.

I do not know of a single parent who does not spend at least some time worrying about their child suddenly dying for no reason. And Raffi had had a heart condition. While he lay next to us in the bassinet, tiny, vulnerable, unpracticed at life, I listened to his breathing. It was raspy, sporadic, sometimes too fast and sometimes too slow. I looked it up on the Mayo Clinic website and they said that this was normal. I was reassured. But I kept listening. Raffi must have been about three years old when I stopped going into his room to check that he was breathing.

As for rocking the baby to keep him from crying while you

write emails or your novel, you can sort of do that, but the trick is that to keep the baby from crying you usually have to pick him up. That makes it harder to write your novel. So does the fact that you are sleeping in two-hour increments. So does the fact that your in-laws have (very helpfully) moved in. In general, there are a lot of things during this period that are conspiring to keep you from writing your novel.

During the first few days of Raffi's life he slept on the bed between me and Emily. I liked having him there so I could hear and feel him breathing. But Emily was convinced I was going to roll over onto him and kill him. So we moved him to a little bassinet next to the bed. Emily would wake multiple times during the night to feed him. I would wake multiple times to look up something online that was worrying me. Raffi's poop was yellow—was that normal? The Mayo Clinic website said yes. No tears came out when he cried—was that OK? (Yes.) Some of the time Emily and I sent each other these factoids over email, since we were taking turns sleeping and didn't necessarily see that much of each other. She sent me a video tutorial on how to give a baby a bath. (Wash his face before he pees in the water!) I sent her a description of infant growth spurts, when they feed (and wake up) more than usual. I also sent her some accounts, from an internet message board, of early baby vomiting: Raffi was spitting up a little, and we wondered what it meant. Nothing, actually. He just had a small stomach.

Later on I would read a brilliant book about parenting advice called *Raising America* by Ann Hulbert. Hulbert had gone back to the early books by American parenting experts, from the end of the nineteenth century, and then read them all sequentially to the present. In the process, she made three remarkable intellectual discoveries. The first was that each generation produced a "hard" and a "soft" parenting guru—in effect they produced each other. The soft guru would tell mothers to listen to their instincts and do what came naturally; the hard guru would chide mothers for their softheartedness and accuse them of spoiling their children. It was fascinating that Hulbert found this pattern over and over (the one exception was during the Dr. Spock hegemony, from the late 1940s to the early '60s; Spock was so dominant he had to become his own "hard" antagonist), but even more fascinating was her next observation: that much of the time the "hard" adviser was actually easier on mothers, because unlike the soft adviser he set some limits on what they were expected to do. Hulbert's final major discovery was about the provenance of parenting advice. I would have thought that experts imposed themselves on parents, but it seems the opposite was true. The first modern parenting advice book, *The Care and Feeding of Children* by L. Emmett Holt, MD, from 1894, began as a handbook on baby care that Holt had written for the nurses at his hospital. The handbook began circulating in samizdat, however, so eager were new mothers to read it. Holt eventually published it properly and sold millions of copies. (Dr. Spock's mother, for one, was an avid Holtian and refused, per Holt's advice, to feed young Spock bananas.) That the experts were not interloping but were essentially invited into American life was one of those things that only made sense to me once I became a parent.

We were desperate for advice. There was a lot of it online, but I also bought two books: the encyclopedic *The Baby Book* by William Sears, MD, guru of the "attachment parenting" school, and *The New Basics* by Michel Cohen, MD, a French-born New York pediatrician, founder of the Tribeca Pediatrics mini-chain, and a critic of attachment parenting. I figured that if we had the attachment guy and the enemy of the attachment guy, we'd be OK. Though we refused to buy the bestselling *The Happiest Baby on the Block* by Harvey Karp, MD, because it seemed corny—we did not want Raffi to be the happiest baby, we wanted him to be the most *interesting* baby—we nonetheless absorbed through some kind of cultural osmosis its clever argument that human children, because of their large heads, are forced out of the womb too early and that the first three months of their lives, when all they do is sleep and wail and eat, should be seen as a "fourth trimester," a time when they ought by all rights to still be in the womb. Given this, the best way to make them stop crying is to simulate the conditions of the womb— keep the baby warm and snug, move him around a lot the way his mother used to, and make shushing sounds to re-create the sound of blood rushing past him. The books we did buy had some good advice as well. I particularly enjoyed Michel Cohen for his wit and his brevity and his belief that Americans worried too much about their children and should be a little tougher on the brats, though Cohen was also a crank who thought that most childhood ailments were imaginary and that to undermine the baby wipe–industrial complex, people should make their own baby wipes at home.

We chose a pediatrician, Dr. E., based on the advice of our midwives, and when Raffi was little we hung on her every word. She seemed to be all that stood between Raffi and death, between us and madness. Overall, she was a warm and nonjudgmental figure in our lives. When Raffi lost a few ounces of weight a week after being born, she told us this was normal and not to worry. And when little Raffi's butt became a bit red and chafed from all the diaper changing, she suggested we use small hospital gauze pads dipped in warm water instead of store-bought wipes. This increased the difficulty of diaper changing by about 30 percent, but it did help Raffi's butt be less chafed.

Beyond that, though, she didn't have much to say. There were too many little things that came up, too many problems here and there. I remember when we saw her for Raffi's two-month checkup: we were about to visit my father on Cape Cod. It was our first long drive with him; we had no idea what to expect, and we told Dr. E. that we were nervous.

"Oh!" she said. "I once had to drive my daughter to the Cape by myself when she was a baby. I spent the whole trip reaching back and trying to comfort her. It was harrowing."

We appreciated the solidarity. Still, our trip to the Cape was absolutely brutal. Raffi screamed the entire way. Every hour or so we would pull over and Emily would feed him. The low point was feeding him in a gas station parking lot in Stamford, Connecticut, cars pulling in and out around us, I-95 rumbling overhead. The four-hour drive took eight hours. When we arrived at last at the Cape, we learned that my father had recently brought home a huge Mongolian wolfhound puppy, and that for the next week we'd have to keep Raffi from getting trampled by him.

A month later we prepared to embark on another long trip, this time to Emily's parents' house, in Maryland. Before going, we happened to visit Eric and Rachael. We told them we were apprehensive about another long drive with Raffi. "Oh," they said. "Do you use the sleep app on your phones?" It turned out there was an app you could download that made various soothing noises, including "loud brook running," that helped kids fall asleep. Or anyway, it had helped their kid fall asleep, and it helped Raffi fall asleep as well. He still screamed and wailed most of the way, but the white noise app gave us an hour, at least, of peace.

FOR MOST OF THE time period covered in this book, we lived in the same one-and-a-half-bedroom apartment above the bar on Franklin Avenue in Bed-Stuy. We were on the third floor; on the second floor, between us and the bar, was our Jamaican landlord, Mr. O., who also owned two small buildings across the street and was enjoying the changes taking place in the neighborhood and the increased rents these portended for his properties. Every year he raised our rent just a little bit more than we would have liked.

Our building was old and the floor of our apartment creaked and groaned when we walked on it, but otherwise the apartment was in good shape. The kitchen was a semi-separate space, with a nice serving hatch, as it's called, to the living room, which made the apartment seem bigger. The windows in the kitchen and living room faced the backyard, which the bar made use of during warm weather until late at night—sometimes as late as four in the morning. We had seen the place on a quiet Monday evening in the fall, when the bar was quiescent; by the standards of the area, the apartment was underpriced. We took it. We moved in a few weeks later, on a Saturday, and when we finally lay down, exhausted, after a day of lugging all our stuff, we could hear the dance music from downstairs coming up violently through the floorboards, the bass shaking the entire building. I had thought our bar was a quiet, seedy dive; I learned on that Saturday that it was in fact a vibrant, exuberant gay bar. At first we were shocked and dismayed, though by the time Raffi was born we had come to love our apartment. We still hated the bar.

The area had once been home to a lot of light industry, with an elevated subway line running through it, and even as the old factories got converted to condos, there were still in our two-block radius some dry goods wholesalers, a woodworking shop, even an auto repair shop. Our block had some touches of gentrification as well as some holdouts: there was a coffee shop where people sat with laptops, a French thin-crust pizzeria, and our bar; on the other hand there was a coin-operated laundromat, a Chinese takeout, and an old-school barbershop. The only wine store in the neighborhood still had bulletproof glass. Guys hung out in front of the barbershop all day and into the evening, drinking out of little pint-size bottles and engaging in loud disputes about the NBA. On the night Raffi was born they were in the middle of one such dispute just as Emily was on our bed, pushing Raffi out, and the guys were being so loud that Martine actually took a moment to look out the window to make sure there wasn't a fight. In fact those guys never fought. The fights happened at the "social club" next door, which was open only a few nights a week and tended to host birthday parties and baby showers—and those, toward the end of the night, would often spill out into the streets and include fistfights and police. They were not having such a party on the night Raffi was born.

We never really knew our neighborhood until Raffi came along. We were strangers there. The locals ignored us and we ignored them. I avoided the barbershop guys and said hello to, but did not really engage with, the young guy who spent hours each day hanging out on the stoop next to ours. We did our laundry, went to the coffee shop with our laptops, occasionally got Chinese takeout, but never lingered anywhere. There was a large, lush community garden at the end of our block, but I had never been in it.

And then came Raffi. Suddenly, the neighborhood opened

up to us. The name of the guy who sat on his stoop was Wood; he was a personal trainer who dreamed of making it big in fashion. The man who ran the laundromat came from China in 1989, in the wake of Tiananmen Square, where he had been a pro-democracy activist. I won't claim that I got to know the barbershop guys, but they did start taking an interest in Raffi when he got a little older and could dance to the music they liked to play from little speakers on the sidewalk. And the very first time we left the house with Raffi, when he was just a few days old, we walked into the open gate of the community garden. In the next four years, we probably spent more time there than at any other place on earth. Raffi became friends with the chickens and once almost drowned in the koi pond.

And we noticed, too, as we never had before, all the parents and their babies. They'd been invisible to me: now they were all I saw. I saw little babies and big babies and cute babies and rich babies (in expensive strollers). We made friends with the people who brought their babies to the community garden and with people on our block who had babies and then, when Raffi was a few months old, with Matt and Emma, who lived around the corner, had grown up not far from Emily, and whose son, E., was a few weeks younger than Raffi. Eventually he and Raffi became best friends, and Matt and Emma became our best parent-friends. She was an avant-garde dance choreographer and he was a designer, and they were probably the only people we knew who had less money than we did. They were great people and great parents, and they helped define and make clear to us our limitations. They had also had a home birth, but they went further than that. They used cloth diapers, owned no paper towels, built most of their own furniture, and eventually took in some chickens (from the community garden) to live in their backyard. They did not employ a nanny or send E. to day care. We were amazed by them, and watching them do what they did brought home to us the realization that we could not do the same.

ONE LEARNED BY WATCHING other parents; by reading; by discussing; by developing ideas and aspirations and then testing them against reality.

A few months before Raffi was born we watched a child-rearing documentary called *Babies*. It has a simple and ingenious premise: the filmmakers follow four babies from different places— San Francisco, Tokyo, rural Mongolia, and rural Namibia—from birth to one year. There is no expert commentary or analysis; you just see what parents and kids do during that time in those places. The results are fascinating. The experiences in Tokyo and San Francisco are pretty similar: a lot of attention given to the baby; at a pretty early age a separate room; baby yoga classes, etc. The Mongolian and Namibian ones are far-out, though. In Mongolia, the baby is tied down in various ways, especially once he learns to crawl, while his parents go out to tend to their flocks. In Namibia, the mother breastfeeds the infant and puts lotion on her head, but otherwise leaves her to her own devices and in the care of her many, many siblings. It is hard to say which baby is happiest, but it is clear which baby develops the fastest and walks the earliest: the Namibian baby, Ponijao. (The Mongolian baby walks last.) For any future parent, the conclusion is obvious: you should raise your baby the Namibian way.

Very soon after Raffi was born I realized this was not going to be possible. For one thing, he did not have eight siblings, or any siblings. In fact, our support from relatives, while enthusiastic, was minimal. My dad lived four hours away and didn't really have any interest in childcare; Emily's parents also lived four hours away, and while they did have an interest in childcare, they also still had jobs. My sibling, Masha, and their wife, Dasha, lived in New York but had three kids of their own, the youngest of them himself still a toddler. Vova, their eldest, was into weight lifting and girls; Yolka, then fourteen, may have had some interest in childcare, but was also quite busy. When she came to see baby Raffi, she was in the throes of the competitive New York City high school admissions process. "In fourteen years," she said, looking at Raffi, "that baby is going to be very stressed out about where he goes to high school."

The differences between us and Ponijao's mom did not end there. In an amazing scene guaranteed to shock and astound Western audiences, baby Ponijao is allowed to lie on the ground and put just about everything imaginable into her mouth, including, at one point, what appears to be some kind of bone. We, too, would have loved to let Raffi crawl around in our community garden and chew on whatever he found there. But he seemed to have a particular talent for finding broken glass and the occasional used condom. We lived in a big city. There were lots of dangers around.

Ponijao's mom always carries her on her body, and some of our friends, Matt and Emma in particular, did the same. But we found the stroller quite convenient and put Raffi in it as soon as it was safe to do so. Matt and Emma also lived in a one-bedroom apartment and had no choice but to sleep in the same bed as E. before moving him to a crib in the same room. Our apartment had a little half bedroom off our room, so at around four months we moved Raffi there. And on it went. In instance after instance, we found that we were living in Brooklyn, not a village in Namibia, and that this made all the difference.

One sort of humiliating moment came when Raffi was about two months old and we were visiting my father. Raffi was not then, nor would he ever be, a good napper. We spent seemingly half our lives swinging and shooshing and swaddling him so that he would fall asleep. My dad, meanwhile, was very excited to have us visiting, very excited to meet his new grandson, and as proof of his excitement he went off to the local Walmart and returned with a gigantic Fisher-Price infant swing. According to the picture on the box it had a cavernous cradle for the baby, massive supports spreading out in several directions, and a huge egg-like thing up top that generated the power for the swing. The box it came in was the size of a coffin. It was the sort of thing that only a man who lived in a huge house in the woods could possibly think would fit in a tiny New York apartment.

Emily said to me, "We can't take that thing home with us."

I said, "I know."

I figured that if I just ignored the box, we could leave it there without anyone noticing. But my teenage half brothers, Daniel and Philip, were curious, and they took the swing out of the box and assembled it. Then it stood there, massive and ugly, in my father's living room. I told my father that it was a great swing but there was no way we could find room for it in our apartment.

"Just put him in it," said my dad of baby Raffi. "Let him decide."

We put Raffi—restless, edgy, sleepless Raffi—into the swing and turned it on, and he immediately fell asleep.

We not only took that swing home, plunking it down in the middle of our living room and rearranging the other furniture around it, but that entire summer we lugged it around with us everywhere we went. We took it to Emily's parents' house. We took it back to my dad's house. We even took it on a short, ill-advised trip to Rhode Island that we arranged with some of our pre-parenting friends. The trip involved a long car ride and then a ferry crossing, and we were there for only three days. Nonetheless, the swing came with us and continued to work its magic.

Eventually, Raffi grew out of the swing, and since it was too huge and ugly to keep around the house in case we had another baby, we gave it away. When Ilya was born, we got a much smaller, more attractive swing, not even a swing but a "rocker"; it was more expensive than the Fisher-Price swing, took up less room, and was far more elegant. It didn't work. Whereas the Fisher-Price really *swung* the baby several feet in each direction, this thing just kind of vibrated and mildly shook. Maybe there were babies for whom this would have worked, but not our babies. I sold the rocker on Craigslist, then went out and got a used giant Fisher-Price swing. Ilya slept happily in it, just as his older brother had.

So we were not living up to our highest parenting ideals. We used disposable diapers and strollers and a very ugly plastic swing. We even got a babysitter. In retrospect I have zero problem with any of these decisions. They reflected our circumstances and they kept us basically sane. But at the time each of them felt like a small defeat, like we didn't have a parenting philosophy, like we didn't know what we were doing.

SLEEP. NOTHING IN OUR lives changed so much as where and how and how much we slept. The giant swing helped with the early naps, but you couldn't keep a kid in it once he learned to roll over (strapped down, he could suffocate). And anyway, it wasn't the naps that were depriving us of sleep: it was the nighttime wakings. Raffi passed two months and then three and four, and still he woke up at least two but sometimes three or four times a night. Emily would feed him and he'd sometimes go back to sleep; other times he would not, and then I'd get up and walk him around and wait for him to settle down. The worry and excitement of the first few weeks had passed. Now Emily and I were just exhausted. We had started referring to him semi-sarcastically as our "treasure." Our treasure who screamed and wailed and pooped and kept us up at night, and whom we missed intolerably the moment he was out of our sight. We were going to have to sleep train him.

There is almost nothing as settled in the parenting literature as sleep training: it works, has no harmful long-term effects, and the only measurable outcome is on the mother's mood, which improves with the increased sleep she receives. It is called "training" because while everyone is born knowing how to sleep, going *back* to sleep when you've woken up in the middle of the night in a room separate from your parents is something you need to learn. And one of the things sleep research discovered long ago is that people, babies and adults both, wake up multiple times a night. As an adult you don't notice it. Babies do notice, however, and often have trouble falling asleep again. This is where the sleep training comes in. Babies need to learn that waking up is OK, that they can just close their eyes again and think of something pleasant and soon sleep will come.

Dr. E. recommended that we read the infamous Richard Ferber, MD, author of *Solve Your Child's Sleep Problems*. He is infamous because of his "method," which involves putting the baby in his crib at bedtime and letting him cry before going in to soothe him; you then gradually increase the amount of time you let him cry until he finally gets bored of crying and goes to sleep. After that, he will be able to go to sleep on his own.

Despite its fearsome reputation, Ferber's book turns out to

be quite gentle. It describes the state of sleep science, explains REM and non-REM sleep as well as baby (and adult) sleep cycles, and suggests some troubleshooting tips for children and sleeping. In a section on children who are afraid of monsters, Ferber writes that "although it may be helpful to show her briefly that the shadows in the closet are in fact shadows and not monsters, it is generally not helpful to get into extended searches of the room or rearranging the furniture during the night." He isn't even that gung-ho about crying—the baby needs to learn how to sleep, he writes, not how to cry. Ferber's main theoretical argument is about "associations"—if the baby associates falling asleep with breastfeeding, he will have trouble falling asleep without breastfeeding; likewise, if he always falls asleep in his parents' bed, he will be puzzled to wake up later in his crib. (Ferber compares it to an adult falling asleep on the couch and then waking up in his bed: you, too, would be confused, at least momentarily, about how you got from one place to the next.) In short, at around four months, we decided to try it. We put Raffi in his crib, let him cry a little bit, went in and soothed him, and then let him cry some more.

It was horrible. We sat in the living room, as far away from him as we were able to get in our small apartment, and also cried. On that first night we went in to him and rocked or fed him to sleep, and on the second night also, after a slightly longer period of crying, but on the third night we held out, and Raffi cried and cried, but eventually he fell asleep. A few hours later, we fell asleep. And then, a few hours after *that*, Raffi woke up again.

Here is where we screwed up, I think. But it was one thing to be strong and rational at seven P.M., sitting on our couch, clutching Ferber's book to our chests, but it was quite another thing at two A.M., with little baby Raffi crying six feet away from us in the half bedroom. He was probably hungry—he was used to eating at this time. And while he would not have starved to death if we hadn't gone in and fed him, it seemed too cruel. I went and got him, and Emily fed him. He went back to sleep. And from there on out, he maybe slept a little bit better. It's possible he woke up less frequently. But we still fed him in the middle of the night. And then as the months went on it turned out there were a number of other reasons he might be waking up at night. He was teething and it hurt; or he had a cold and was uncomfortable. On those occasions, we would go in. On other occasions, we would try to let him cry. In short, it seemed like sleep training was a spell that wore off; every few months we'd have to do it again. Clearly, we had done something wrong, were doing something wrong. But we couldn't manage to do better. He was so vulnerable, and so precious, and also it didn't help that he was never more than a few feet away. The one time he actually slept through the entire night was when we were visiting my dad, and Raffi's room was a decent distance from ours, and also we had a very loud dehumidifier in our room. Maybe he cried, maybe he didn't; we had no idea because we couldn't hear him.

We called it the Miracle of the Cape. When we got back home to Brooklyn, he started waking up again, and we heard him.

Was sleep training our greatest failure as parents? Certainly it caused us a lot of grief, and not just in those first few months. Raffi kept waking up, and when we moved him (too early) to a toddler bed, he started coming into our bed. From the age of two and a half to five, no matter where we were on the planet, no matter what bed Raffi was in, at two A.M. he would come and find us. Sometimes I would carry him back to his bed; other times I would let him sleep with us. He would often spend the night turning this way and that and occasionally kicking us. But it was better than having to keep waking up and carrying him back again. Sometimes, too, he was quiet and angelic in our bed; and sometimes he would have a nightmare, and in those instances it was nice to be able to comfort him right away.

At one point, when Raffi was nearing three, the extended bedtimes and the nighttime visits became so bad that we hired a sleep specialist to help us, though not before having a big argument over the expense. The sleep specialist, Dr. K., looked at our layout, sized us up as wussbags, and explained how to change our bedtime routine so that Raffi would get to bed earlier. She also said that since we were clearly not willing to just close the door to Raffi's room and lock it, we could at least put in a child gate, so that he could see us but not reach us in the middle of the night. When, a few weeks later, Raffi figured out how to open the gate, Dr. K. told us to secure the gate with a zip tie, then cut it off in the morning. "Don't apologize for being parents," she told us sternly.

It was such good advice! It was great advice. But what "being parents" actually meant (aside from zip-tying the gate, which we did, and it worked, until Raffi figured out how to climb over it, at which point we gave up)—well, that was not so simple.

THOSE FIRST TWO YEARS, but especially the first year, were the years of Emily. She had delivered Raffi into the world and then kept him alive with her body. She knew how to calm him down when he was upset, and she could frequently infer what ailed him just from the timbre of his cries. I did my best to show that I was also a competent parent—I would pick him up when he cried, carry him around, change his diaper—but it was no contest. If something was really wrong, if Raffi was choking or in pain or just inconsolable for some mysterious reason, I would find myself handing him to Emily. She alone could fix it.

And it wasn't just the Raffi-handling stuff. Emily was social. She is a writer with a sharp and critical eye, she can be very cutting, but as a person out in the world she is nice. She never wants to leave a conversation when she's run into someone, even someone she doesn't know that well. In the months after Raffi was born, Emily quickly assembled a network of mothers who could offer advice and comfort, hand down clothes, and otherwise lighten our burden. What we lacked in relatives we soon made up for in friends, specifically Emily's friends.

It was through a friend of Emily's named Rebecca that we solved one of life's great mysteries: babysitting. At the time I simply couldn't understand how we would manage to leave our precious child in the hands of a total stranger, just so that we could work. People did it all the time, but it made no sense. What kind of interview, what sort of questionnaire, what battery of tests would you have to come up with to make you feel like it was something you could do?

The answer was very simple: you trusted the people whom people you trusted had trusted. Rebecca had two daughters a few years older than Raffi, and they had been cared for from an early age by a young woman named Asia. Asia! She was a striking woman, six foot two, with high-end cosmetics and a different wig for every day of the week. She was great with babies. When Raffi was four months old, we started leaving him with her. I remember the first time Emily and I left the house together without him. We walked out onto Franklin, unencumbered by a diaper bag or stroller or Raffi himself. It was liberating and it was terrifying. I went to a café and spent one hour working and two hours worrying. Asia sent photos of Raffi lying on his play mat and then sleeping. The next day I spent two hours working and one hour worrying. Before long we turned the three hours into four hours, and then five hours, and eventually it was eight. For the next year, until he started day care, Raffi spent almost as much time with Asia, and another little girl she started watching, as he did with us.

FOR THE FIRST SIX MONTHS of Raffi's life, we had a small amount of savings and no income. We paid our rent, put a lot of stuff on our credit card, and tried not to spend too much money. In December of that year, I finally sold *A Terrible Country*, the novel that I'd been writing, on and off, for six years, and that I would work on for another two. That gave us a little bit of breathing room. The next year, after surveying our finances and realizing that they were unsustainable, I started applying for teaching jobs. Somewhat miraculously, I got one. This stabilized our finances, though it didn't change the fact that we were living in a city full of bankers and corporate lawyers and "start-up entrepreneurs" who were making far, far more than we were. We were reminded of this daily.

Having a baby altered how I thought about money. Before Raffi, there was nothing that people with more money had that I actually wanted. Now there was. Our friends with money could and did hire infinite childcare, including at night. Some sent their kids to private school. They never worried about their landlord complaining about the noise they were making, because they lived in their own houses. Our lack of money, which had been if not a virtue of ours then at least not harmful to anyone, was now denying our child things that other children had. It felt unfair to him. But he was stuck with us.

Emily and I had always fought about money. After Raffi was born, we opened a brand-new front in our fighting: housework. Emily had never particularly liked the fact that I was a messy person who left books and printouts all over the house, but she had tolerated it. Now things were different. We had a new roommate who was very messy; he was also very demanding.

(He was so demanding at mealtimes that we started calling him "Mr. Baby," as in "We're sorry this dinner doesn't meet your standards, Mr. Baby.") Some chores that were once considered onerous became almost desirable if they involved leaving the house. Emily started to grow suspicious of my long trips to the laundromat—did we really produce so much laundry, or was I just trying to get away?

I thought frequently of Phyllis Rose's summary, in *Parallel Lives*, of the marriage of Thomas Carlyle and Jane Welsh. They may have been miserable; they may have fought constantly; "but they were certainly a couple." We were certainly a couple. "To say that they clashed in many ways," Rose writes, "and in many ways disappointed each other is to say no more than that they were married, and for a long time."

Of Emily I can honestly say that there was no one I more admired, no one whose insight into our children I more eagerly sought, no one who could light up a room as she did. She was beautiful, and that made it easier. But it didn't make it easy.

AND WHAT WAS RAFFI LIKE? For the first few weeks he was just tiny and vulnerable; that was all we knew of him. We monitored his breathing, his eating; we looked up the colors of his poops online. But pretty soon he began to evince a personality. In short, he began to scream. In the early evenings in our Franklin Avenue apartment, the screaming would begin. He was not hungry, wet, uncomfortable, or anything else we could address.

He was, perhaps, tired, but not yet ready to go to sleep. In the parenting literature this screaming has a name: colic. But what it actually is, and what causes it, is under dispute. Our two parenting books—Sears and Cohen—were, as usual, at loggerheads. Sears calls colic "heart breaking" and attributes it—potentially— to "transient lactase deficiency," and blames it on the mother's diet. He has a long list of foods, including chicken, eggs, and tomatoes, that mothers should avoid while breastfeeding. Pretty soon, for just this sort of advice, Emily would banish Sears from our home, but at the time I thought, "Is Emily eating something that is causing our baby's tummy to hurt? Is she *poisoning* our baby?" I can't remember, but I may have brought it up to her.

Michel Cohen has a very different view on colic. "As far as I'm concerned," Cohen writes, "colic does not really exist." He does not deny that there are some babies who cry more than others, but he rejects the idea that there is some "normal" amount of crying that babies should be allowed to do, and he thinks it is nonsense to suggest that their crying is caused by the mother's diet or a failed uptake of lactose or some other Searsian mumbo jumbo. (The Mayo Clinic states simply that there is no known cause of colic.) For Cohen, the crying is caused by what Karp calls "the fourth trimester"—the baby's pained adaptation to life outside the womb. Everything else is superstition. "I have encountered nursing mothers who literally eat white rice all day, fearing that any other nutrient will be too harsh on their baby's tummy," he writes. "But it's an old wives' tale that your diet has anything to do with his crying process."

So Raffi would scream and he would refuse to stop for exactly one hour. Despite Cohen's admonition that we shouldn't worry about it, we worried about it; then we tried to tolerate it; then we figured out that if I picked him up and took him outside for a walk, he would settle down. So that's what we started doing. I would take him out for an evening stroll up Franklin and over to Bedford, and people would admire him and ask to look at him. He'd stop crying. And then, as Cohen had predicted, the screaming eventually ended at around four months.

It is so hard to disentangle our nervousness from Raffi's. What was the motor: His fussiness, his heart condition, which we still hadn't forgotten about, his screaming—or our fears? Which caused which? It's impossible to tell. But our fears came first, of course: during the pregnancy, during the birth classes, during the birth itself. Perhaps we passed them down to Raffi; perhaps they had nothing to do with us at all.

He was a sensitive baby, and he grew into a sensitive toddler, and he is now a sensitive boy. The world is not something he can ignore; it impinges on him; he sees it and hears it and feels it deeply. This has not always been easy for his somewhat less sensitive father to understand.

That he is sensitive does not mean that he is quiet or peaceful. From an early age Raffi has liked to wrestle, and crash into things, and run away, so that we will chase after him. As soon as we got out the door and onto the sidewalk, he would take off. The thing to do, according to the literature, would be to not chase after him. Sometimes Wood, who sat on the stoop next to our building, would step out and catch him. But sometimes Raffi ran in the other direction, and what if he ran out into the street? There were a lot of cars speeding by. *Probably* he wouldn't run out into the street. But what if he did? So we ignored the literature and ran.

In the end, there was no piece of advice, no matter how wise or well meaning, that could penetrate to the core of our particular situation. Billions of parents throughout human history had gone through what we were going through—but not in quite the same way, with the same resources, on the same street, with the same family backgrounds, and most of all, not with this particular child. All happy families are alike, says Tolstoy, while each unhappy family is unhappy in its own way. Was this the case? Were we an unhappy family? There were many times when it seemed like it. But also there were times when it did not. And as for happy families, the ones that resemble all other happy families—I'm not sure we ever met one.

There was no family like ours and no child like ours. He liked dressing up and pretending to be a Teenage Mutant Ninja Turtle—he would take the changing pad off the dresser, strap it to his back, then pick up his little hockey stick and use it as a sword. He said that if a giant came to our house, he would push him out the window. When he was little, and we were visiting my father on the Cape, he liked to take his clothes off and splash in the shallow waves. "Dada, I'm a crab and I'm going to pinch you!" He was Max from *Where the Wild Things Are*. He did not have a wolf suit, but he did have a monster suit, and he would put it on and chase our cat, Swizzle, around the apartment, sometimes with a knife. But we were not like Max's mother, who for his misbehavior sends Max to bed without his supper. The idea of us depriving Raffi of his supper was inconceivable. We were nervous, crazy, middle-class parents, and he was our firstborn child.

Say It in Russian

I don't remember when exactly I started speaking Russian to Raffi. It wasn't when he was in the womb, though I've since learned that this is when babies first start recognizing sound patterns. And I didn't speak to him in Russian in the first few weeks of his life; it felt ridiculous to do so. All he could do was sleep and scream and breastfeed, and really the person I was talking to when I talked to him was his mother, who was sleep-deprived and on edge and needed company. Emily does not know Russian.

But then, at some point, I started. It turned out I liked the feeling, when I carried him through the neighborhood or pushed him in his stroller, of having our own private language. "Did you see that baby?" I would say in Russian. "That was a cute baby." I liked the number of endearments to which Russian gave me access. *Mushkin, mazkin, glazkin, moy horoshy, moy lyubimy, moy malen'ky mal'chik.* It is a language surprisingly rich in endearments, given its history. And to me it was the language of childhood, the language of love for children, the language in which my parents and grandmothers had spoken to me.

When we started reading books to Raffi, I included some

Russian ones. A friend had handed down a beautiful book of Daniil Kharms's poems for children, illustrated by the Russian artist Igor Oleynikov; the poems are not nonsense verse, but they are pretty close, and to my surprise Raffi enjoyed them. I enjoyed them too. *"Ivan Ivanych Samovar / byl puzaty samovar / trekh-vederny samovar"* went the first poem—"Ivan Ivanovich Samovar / was a pot-bellied samovar / a three-bucket samovar." And then the poem tells the story of how various members of a family come and get some tea from the samovar, until finally little Denis wants some tea, but there is none left, because he has slept too late! There is a poem about two dogs who make a mess in an artist's studio, and another about three little kids pretending to be a car, a postal steamship, and a "Soviet airplane," respectively. Kharms was a member of the OBERIU poets, an avant-garde group in 1920s Leningrad; he was a genius and an eccentric. He was not anti-Soviet, exactly, but he was attuned to the horrors of the age and couldn't prevent them from seeping into his work. In 1937, the bloodiest year of the Stalinist purges, Kharms published a poem in *The Hedgehog*, a popular children's magazine. It is about a man who leaves his house with a walking stick and a sack. In Eugene Ostashevsky and Matvei Yankelevich's translation:

A man once walked out of his house
With a walking stick and a sack
    And on he went

And on he went
He never did turn back.

He walked as far as he could see:
He saw what lay ahead.
He never drank,
He never slept,
Nor slept nor drank nor ate.

Then once upon a morning
He entered a dark wood
And on that day,
And on that day
He disappeared for good.

If anywhere by any chance
You meet him in his travels,
Then hurry please,
Then hurry please,
Then hurry please and tell us.

The poem was apparently about Kharms's dream of escaping the big city, but it could also be read as an allegory about the purges. Apparently some people did so read it, because Kharms stopped being published. He stopped receiving payments due from his publisher, and he and his wife began to starve. "Here is how hunger begins," he writes, in Robert Chandler's translation:

> first you wake in good cheer,
> then weakness begins,
> and then boredom,
> and then comes the loss
> of the power of swift reason
> and then comes calm—
> and then the horror.

Kharms was finally arrested in 1941, once the war had begun, and died in the psych ward of the famous Kresty Prison in February 1942, probably of starvation.

In the book of Kharms's poems from which I read to Raffi, none of this was indicated. The poem about the man who disappears was in the middle of the book, and I would sing it; I happened to know the tune because the Soviet bard Alexander Galich, one of the culture heroes I had inherited from my parents, had written a song about Kharms's arrest in which he embedded the lyrics of the poem about the man who leaves the house. I felt its whole strange, tragic history in my chest as I sang it to Raffi, but Raffi of course had no idea. In any case, he really liked it. When he got old enough to request what I read to him, at around two, he would request that song and then dance.

As with a lot of my parenting decisions, I hadn't really thought this one through. Why was I doing this, exactly? I didn't have any elderly relatives who spoke only Russian. My father was now the oldest person in our family, and while he was more comfortable with Russian than English, he'd been living in the United States for over thirty years and his English was very good. Even my favorite aunt, Aunt Sveta, who lived in Moscow, spoke very reasonable English. I remember a friend of mine urging me, before Raffi was born, to speak Russian to him. I found it annoying. If my friend wanted someone to speak Russian to Raffi, he could do it himself. But my friend didn't know Russian. My few Russian friends, meanwhile, did not offer that opinion. They knew that a language was not just a set of words, but a culture and a history—one that most of us, for various reasons, had wanted to escape.

For the first weeks and months of speaking Russian to Raffi, I felt like a person who was pretending to speak Russian to Raffi. He didn't understand me. Emily didn't understand me. I could have been speaking anything and just claiming that it was Russian. It was just a bunch of sounds.

But then, at around one, I saw him beginning to understand. We started with animal sounds. "What does a cow"—*korova*—"say?" I would ask. "Moo!" Raffi would answer. "What does a *koshka* say?" "Meow." "And what does an owl"—*sova*—"say?"

Raffi would make his eyes big and raise his arms and pronounce, "Hoo, hoo." At a certain point, maybe a few months later, he seemed to learn that *nyet* meant "no"—I said it a lot. (Emily said she was also picking up the Russian for "That's not food!" and "That's not a toy!"—*Eto ne eda! Eto ne igrushka!*) He didn't understand me as well as he understood his mother, and he didn't understand either of us all that much, but still it felt like a minor miracle. I had given my son some Russian! After that, I felt I had to keep going. It helped of course that people were so supportive and impressed. "It's wonderful that you're teaching him Russian," they said. Well, maybe.

I read up on bilingualism. It turns out that the question of whether it was good or bad for you was first mooted at the start of the twentieth century in the context of intelligence testing and the eugenics movement. In the U.S., much intelligence testing was done on immigrant populations; one infamous study, carried out at Ellis Island in 1913 by the eugenicist Henry Goddard, concluded that between 40 and 83 percent of the Jewish immigrants tested were "feeble-minded." (Goddard himself was surprised, or pretended to be surprised, by the results, but then explained that since these immigrants were coming later than other immigrants, it stood to reason that they were, genetically, "the poorest of [their] race.") These tests led to a robust debate over whether the immigrants not knowing English may have had something to do with their scoring poorly on the tests. As the linguist Kenji Hakuta summarizes the history in his excellent book, *The Mirror of Language: The Debate on Bilingual-*

ism, the eugenicist-hereditarians insisted that their intelligence tests were valid despite the language barriers; some of their opponents in the psychological community, meanwhile, who wanted to emphasize the environmental aspects of intelligence, came up with the theory that trying to learn two languages was actually the cause of the problem. As Hakuta points out, neither group considered the possibility that the tests themselves were bogus.

In the early 1960s, the reigning hypothesis that bilingualism was bad for you was debunked by Canadian researchers in the midst of debates over Quebecois nationalism. A study by two McGill University researchers, which used French–English bilingual schoolchildren in Montreal as subjects, found that they actually *outperformed* monolingual children on tests that required mental manipulation and reorganization of visual patterns. Thus was born "the bilingual advantage."

In recent years, the bilingual advantage hypothesis has itself been debunked, at least partially. The McGill study and subsequent ones have been criticized for selection bias—the bilingual schoolchildren in Montreal came from highly educated families. The results have not been replicated. It's possible there is no bilingual advantage, aside from the advantage of knowing another language. And while it is not the case, as some parents still think, that learning another language alongside English will impede English learning significantly, it may be the case that it impedes it a little bit. As the psycholinguist François Grosjean stresses, language is the product of necessity. If a child discusses, say, hockey only with his Russian-speaking father, he may not learn until later how to say "puck" in English. In that sense the Russian version of the word will have displaced the English word, at least temporarily.

Learning that bilingualism was not an automatic advantage, that I was not setting up Raffi for easy admission to the university of his choice, was useful in once again framing the question: Did I like what I was doing? Did I want to be doing it? I watched friends in a similar situation to mine—that is, friends who came over when they were little and still spoke Russian with their parents—decide *not* to speak Russian with their kids. They were more comfortable in English, and that, for them, was the decisive factor. But it also felt to me like they were liberating themselves from Russia, from all its problems and its dangers. It felt like they were finishing the work their parents had begun. I envied them their certainty. I wondered if they were right.

My parents took me out of the Soviet Union in 1981. They did it because they didn't like the Soviet Union, and they did it because there was an opportunity—the U.S. Congress, under pressure from American Jewish groups, had passed legislation that tied U.S.–Soviet trade to Jewish emigration. Leaving wasn't easy, but if you were aggressive and entrepreneurial—my father at one point paid a significant bribe—you could get out. Probably no other decision has had more of an effect on my life.

Despite their emigration, my parents remained attached to Russia in a thousand different ways: the books they read, the people they hung out with, the music they listened to. Somewhere around 1985, we bought a car with a cassette deck. From there on out, whenever we drove anywhere farther than a few miles, we listened to the 1960s bards: tragic Galich, honey-voiced Okudzhava, and angry Vysotsky—above all, Vysotsky. Most of the recordings we owned were made during live concerts Vysotsky had performed; it was just him and a guitar. His raspy voice, his songs about Soviet life, his occasional coughing fits, were the soundtrack of our car trips. For a long time I couldn't make out the words, but eventually they came into focus. My favorite songs were about the war, that is, World War II. There was one in particular I liked about a professor's son named Seryozha Fomin who had supposedly, according to the narrator of the song, stayed home in Moscow and had a great time during the war; at the end of the song he learns that Fomin has in fact received a medal for his service to the motherland, apparently because the narrator has had him all wrong.

So our parents lived in this Russian cocoon, both because they had to and because they wanted to. They weren't incurious about America—they loved America—but they also liked the music they liked and the books they read. My mother was a literary critic who worked at the Russian Research Center at Harvard—it was her job, as well as her inclination, to keep up with events back home.

But it was not our job, the kids' job, nor was it our inclination. We assimilated. I was six when we came over, which meant that though I knew no English I learned it very quickly and spoke it without an accent when I did. (For Russian, age nine or ten seems to be the cutoff; after that, it becomes hard to shed the accent.) For a month at the start of first grade I was in an ESL class, and then they let me go. Within a year I was more comfortable in English than in Russian. But we continued to speak it at home. We knew at least one family who had switched to English, so that the parents could learn the language faster. That was considered déclassé. It was a mark of distinction to be able to speak good Russian. When I was ten my parents started worrying that my Russian was deteriorating and signed me up for a class with a Russian tutor, along with two of my friends; I found it boring and a little humiliating to be doing first-grade grammar at the age of ten, but I did learn the cases, and my spelling improved. My written Russian is still not great, but without that intervention, it would be considerably worse.

As I assimilated further into American life, spent less time with my parents and more with my friends, my Russian continued to decline. I found myself increasingly embarrassed by these strange people, my parents, with their accents, their clothing, their Soviet inability to follow the rules. That Russian people dressed so differently from the natives was something of a miracle, given that they got their clothes at American stores. And now, of course, I am embarrassed at my embarrassment. These lovely people, born in poverty in an annihilated country, steeped in literature but not in fashion, who came to the promised land but could not really taste its fruits: they did it for us, for me, and I had the gall to make fun of them.

It felt like my parents were giving me mixed signals: Russia was great, and Russia was terrible. After all, though we spoke Russian, read Russian, listened to Russian music, we had left Russia and weren't going back. Of the two messages they sent— Russia great; Russia terrible—I decided to heed the second one. That my parents could not assimilate fully to American life did not mean that I should not. I stopped reading in Russian. I refused to listen to Russian music. With my Russian friends I spoke in English. I became, in short, an *amerikanets*—an American.

It took my mother dying of breast cancer for me to start taking Russian seriously. She was first diagnosed with it when I was fifteen. She broke the news to me while we were walking in the woods in a small college town in Vermont; for a few years, my mother went there during the summer to teach Russian literature, something she really enjoyed and that represented a reward of sorts for years of hard work. On this day she told me that she had been diagnosed with an *opukhol'*, but that the doctors had caught it and that she would be undergoing treatment. It sounded bad, but I did not know what an *opukhol'* was, and I was too embarrassed to ask.

Later that day, my father followed up with me. Did my mother tell me the news?

Yes, I said, and then, trying to look on the bright side, I added, "At least it's not cancer."

My father stopped. "It is cancer," he said.

"An *opukhol'* is cancer?"

"Yes," he said. *Opukhol'* means tumor. My mother had a tumor in her breast.

Two years later—years of suffering, chemotherapy, optimistic moments followed by rapid deterioration—she was gone. In addition to everything else that this represented, it was the severing of my strongest connection to Russia and the Russian language. My mom had been the one who had found me the Russian tutor, who'd tried to interest me in Russian books, who'd taken us to Russian movies when they came to town. It was after she died that I realized how far I had let my Russian go. I realized, too, that I could no longer take Russian for granted; if I didn't make an effort to keep it up, it would disappear. When I got to college a year later, I decided, as a kind of homage to my mother, to take Russian literature classes. After that, I went to Moscow for a year. And for the next twenty years I kept going back: as a journalist; as a translator; as the caretaker of my grandmother, my mother's mother, whose only child my mother had been.

My father, for his part, had mixed feelings about all this travel to Russia. When I was over there, he loved coming to visit; he himself, after the Soviet Union fell apart, had a kind of Russian renaissance and started doing business in Russia. But I also remember the expression on his face when he dropped me off at the airport the first time I went over. My sibling, Masha, had gone back to live and work as a journalist a few years earlier. Now I was going too. Was he losing both his kids—to

Russia? Had he, in the absence of my mom, totally screwed up? Aside from my mother's funeral, that parting at the airport was the closest I had seen my father come to crying.

So there is another choice one could make regarding Russian and Russia, and that is to turn one's back on it. One could argue that in teaching Russian to Raffi, I am putting him in danger—I am putting him in danger of going to Russia. And one could also argue that my attempts have been comical. My own Russian is not very good! My grammar is full of holes and so is my vocabulary. For a long time I was calling Raffi's *soska* (pacifier) his *sosul'ka* (lollipop). One time I called his *samokat* (scooter) a *samogon*—moonshine. I feel happy and comfortable speaking Russian to Raffi, but with others, as one mom in a similar situation to mine once put it to me on the playground, I feel constrained. She compared it to being unable to move freely around a room. The Russian word is *skovanny*.

The most intense émigré Russian speakers that I know of are the White Russians of Long Island, who fled the revolution in 1917 and have been keeping their kids learning Russian into the fourth generation. The journalist Paul Klebnikov came from this community. After the Soviet Union fell apart, he started going back to Moscow as a correspondent for *Forbes*. He published a passionate book in the 1990s about the corruption of the Russian state by big business; he published another one a few years later about the dangers of the Chechen mafia to "Russian civilization." The books were uniquely impassioned—reading them, one felt that Klebnikov was writing not as a Western journalist who happened to know Russian, but *as a Russian*. In 2003, he was named editor of Russian *Forbes* and moved to Moscow full time. The next year, while walking to the subway from work, he was shot four times and died. A poorly conducted trial ended in a not-guilty verdict for the two defendants. To this day, he remains the only American journalist assassinated in Moscow. No one has been punished for his murder.

DURING THE FIRST TWO and a half years of Raffi's life, the development of his Russian was pretty halting. His first word was "kika," by which he meant "chicken" (for the chickens in our community garden). For a while, because he used *k* rather than *ch* to start the word, I thought it might be a combination of "chicken" and the Russian word, *kuritza*. But none of his subsequent approximations of words—"ba" for "bottle," "kakoo" for "cracker," "magum" for "mango," "mulk" for "milk"—had any Russian components. A glossary we compiled during a long car trip to visit his grandparents when he was almost eighteen months old identified fifty-three words or attempted words, only one of which had any trace of Russian: "mech," i.e., *myach*, i.e., "ball," presumably because I was the one who was always trying to get him to play ball with me. In retrospect, I had to admit that he said "kika" not because he was trying to say *kuritza*, but because he couldn't pronounce *ch*.

Despite all my qualms about Russian, I was by this point

speaking a lot of it to him, and his failure to learn it was hard not to take personally. Did Raffi prefer the language of his mother (and everyone else around him) to that of his father? Was I—this is probably closer to the truth—not spending enough time with him? Did he sense my ambivalence about the whole project? Did he hate me?

François Grosjean, in his summary of contemporary research in his 2010 book, *Bilingual: Life and Reality*, says that there are three major factors that determine whether a child will learn a second language. The first is need: Does the child have any actual cause to figure out the language, whether it's to speak to relatives or playmates or to understand what's on TV? The second is the volume of "input": Does he hear enough of it to begin to understand? A third factor, more subjective than the others, is the parents' attitude toward the language. Grosjean uses the example of Belgian parents whose children are supposed to learn both French and Flemish; many parents have a less than enthusiastic attitude toward Flemish, not exactly a world language, and their children end up not learning it very well.

In our case, there was absolutely zero need for Raffi to learn Russian—I didn't feel like pretending I couldn't understand his fledgling attempts to speak English, and neither was there anyone else in his life who didn't know English. I did my best to create a reasonable volume of Russian for him, but it was dwarfed by the volume of English. Finally, I had, as I've indicated, a bad attitude.

And yet I kept it up—out of inertia, or stubbornness, or just curiosity. When Raffi was really small, the only Russian books he enjoyed were the nonsense poems by Kharms and the cute 1980s Swedish books about Max by Barbro Lindgren, which Masha had brought me from Moscow in a Russian translation. But around the age of two he started to enjoy the poems of Korney Chukovsky. I had found these too violent and scary (and long) to read to him when he was very little, but as he became somewhat violent himself, and also able to listen to longer stories, we read about Barmaley, the cannibal who eats small children and is friendly with hippopotamuses but is eventually eaten by a crocodile, and then we moved on to the kinder-hearted Dr. Aybolit ("Dr. Ouch"), who takes care of animals and makes a heroic journey to Africa at the invitation of a hippopotamus to cure some sick hippos, tigers, and sharks. (Hippopotamuses were a prominent feature of Chukovsky stories; he believed it was the hippo, rather than the lion, who was king of the jungle.) I also put a few Russian cartoons into his TV rotation—most were too old and too slow for him to like, but there was one that he enjoyed about a melancholy crocodile, Gena, who sings a sad birthday song for himself.

As the months went on I could see that he understood more and more of what I was saying. Not that he did what I told him to do, but sometimes I would mention, for example, my *tapochki*, my slippers, and he would know what I was talking about. One time he hid one of my slippers. "*Gde moy vtoroy tapochek?*" I asked him. Where is my other slipper? He went under the couch and produced it very proudly. And I was also proud. Was our child a genius? Just from my repeating the same words enough times, and pointing to objects, he had learned the Russian words for those objects. It was incredible what the human mind was capable of. I couldn't stop now.

Grosjean's book pointed me to one of the foundational texts in the study of bilingualism, Werner F. Leopold's *Speech Development of a Bilingual Child: A Linguist's Record*, and I took all four volumes out of the university library. It turned out to be an amazing book. Leopold, a German-born linguist, came to the U.S. in the 1920s and eventually got a job teaching German at Northwestern. He married an American woman from Wisconsin; she had German roots but did not know the language, and when, in 1930, they had a daughter, Hildegard, Leopold decided to teach her German on his own. He kept a painstaking record of the results and published *Speech Development* in English over the course of a decade. The first three volumes are quite technical. Volume 1, *Vocabulary Growth in the First Two Years*, begins with the following remarkable paragraph about the language of infancy: "During the first few weeks, the only sounds produced were cries of dissatisfaction. The crying consisted of front vowels between [æ] and [a], usually [a]. During the first week it was clearly [ˀaˡˀaːː], later as a rule simple long [ˀaː]." But the fourth volume is less technical. It is Leopold's personal diary from the time Hildegard turned two.

The book is full of cute grammatical mistakes made by Hildegard, many of them in German, and also a fair number of

technical transcriptions of her German speech. Leopold repeatedly laments the decline of Hildegard's German. "Her German
continues to recede," he writes when she is a little past two. A
few months later: "The progress in German is small. . . . The
displacement of German words by English ones progresses
slowly but steadily." He complains bitterly that he gets no support from his fellow German émigrés: "It is very difficult to
have the influence of the German language reinforced by our
many friends who speak German," he writes. "All of them lapse
involuntarily into English when Hildegard answers in English." When Hildegard goes away with her mother for a week,
Leopold reads the only previous linguistic work about a child's
bilingual development, the French linguist Jules Ronjat's *Le dével-
oppement du langage observé chez un enfant bilingue*. Ronjat,
while raising his daughter in Paris with a German mother, spoke
French to her while his wife spoke German. (They apparently
also had German-speaking childcare help.) The girl learned both
well. But Leopold, like all parents, finds that Ronjat's situation
is not the same as his. "His child learned early to speak the two
languages separately," Leopold notes. "Conditions are not so
favorable in Hildegard's case. The two languages [German and
English] are more closely related, thus not so easy to keep apart.
The language of the mother agrees with that of the environment, so that English is heavily favored. The language foreign
to the environment is not supported by the continuous influence
of nurses speaking that language." There was even here perhaps

a bit of class rage. If only Leopold could afford to hire some German nannies, surely Hildegard's German would improve!

At the same time, one senses in Leopold a beautiful serenity about Hildegard's progress, because she is so cute. "It is surprising that she says *to shave* in English," he writes, "although I am the only one whom she sees shaving. She asks me every time what I am doing and receives the answer in German, 'rasieren.' One evening she touched my beard stubbles and said 'you must shave?'" A few months later he notes that Hildegard has begun to be curious about the two languages she is learning. She asks her mother if all fathers speak German. "Apparently," Leopold notes, "she has up to now tacitly assumed that German is the language of fathers, because it is that of her father. The question reveals the first doubt concerning the correctness of the generalization."

Sometimes her yearning for German things even annoys Leopold a little. "For the last week she has had a passion for the abominable German children's book 'Struwwelpeter.' All day she runs after me with the book and wants me to read to her." He adds in a footnote: "Mark Twain has published a free English adaptation of it. . . . All German children have loved it for over a hundred years in spite of (or because of?) its crudeness and transparent moralizing."

Leopold seems overall like a good father—a good-enough father that he has instilled a love for Germany in his daughter, or at least has communicated that he himself wants to go there. "She has the desire to learn German," he writes, "because she would like to be taken along to Germany some time. Once she offered me her entire wealth of ten cents to enable me to pay for the journey. 'Papa, now have you enough money to go to Germany?'" One deduces from notes like this that the Leopolds were not rich.

Eventually, the family does go to Germany for six months. It is 1935 and Hildegard is four years old; she brags about the trip to her playmates, with baleful results. "The other day she shouted repeatedly *Heil, Hitler!* with a raised arm," writes Leopold. "She did not learn it at home. An older neighbor boy, who speaks only English, had demonstrated it to her as a joke." Leopold is clearly no fan of the Nazi regime, but he wants to visit his father in Hamburg, and he wants Hildegard's German to improve.

It does so *immediately*. Leopold leaves to work for six weeks as a "cultural adviser and interpreter" for a group of American tourists traveling through Germany, Austria, and Switzerland, and after two weeks his wife joins him; as a result, Hildegard spends four weeks with her monolingual German grandfather and aunt. Upon his return, Leopold is amazed and delighted:

We returned on August 21 late at night. When she [Hildegard] awoke the next morning, she greeted us with a friendly smile and started at once to chatter lustily—all in German! The German was by no means good, but complete ability of self-expression and fluency were achieved. The vocabulary was quite comprehensive. Only grammatical accuracy was missing. It was a strange feeling. It did not seem to be our child who chatted so cheerfully in German.

What is more, as Leopold discovers, she has basically forgotten English. She speaks it with her mother with difficulty. It's a bit of a cruel joke, actually—Leopold spends all that time trying to teach Hildegard the language, and then as soon as he leaves her in Germany for a little while, it happens automatically.

And I thought, reading this, that if Werner Leopold could take his daughter to Hitler's Germany so she could learn the language, surely I could take Raffi to Putin's Russia for a little while? But I haven't, yet.

About a month before his third birthday, Raffi's Russian development suddenly accelerated. He began to notice that I was speaking a different language from everyone else—that he was "facing two languages," as Leopold said of Hildegard. Raffi's first reaction was annoyance. "Dada," he said one evening, "we need to put English in you." He clearly conceived of language—correctly, according to Grosjean—as a substance that fills a vessel. I asked him why he couldn't speak Russian to me. "I can't," he said simply. "Mama put English in me."

One night, when Emily and I were talking while putting him to bed, he noticed something strange: "Dada, you speak English to Mama!" He had not noticed it before.

Then his mother went away for a few days and it was just me and him. For the first time since he was conscious of the difference, he was hearing more Russian than English. He began to get the hang of it. "Dada," he exclaimed one evening as he was riding my shoulders home from day care, "this is what it sounds like when I speak Russian." He proceeded to make a series of guttural noises that did not at all sound like Russian. But at least he knew it was a different language. "Dada," he nonetheless insisted, "you have to speak English." "*Pochemu*?" I asked. Why? He answered: "Because I speak English."

But then he started having more fun. "Fee-fi-fo-fum," he chanted one evening, pretending to be a giant, "I smell the blood of a Englishman!" He made as if he were going to eat me. "Me?" I said, in Russian. "I'm an Englishman?" Raffi the giant took the point and adjusted. "I smell the blood," he chanted, "of a Russian man!" He laughed riotously—he loved replacing one word or sound with another. A few weeks later, at dinner, it was something else. I had been speaking to Raffi but then changed the subject and addressed Emily. Raffi didn't like it. "No, Mama!" he said to her. "Don't take Dada's Russian from him!" He wanted me to continue speaking to him—in Russian— rather than ignoring him and speaking to Emily. Russian in this instance stood in for my attention, which he did not want to lose.

We were really in it now. Not only did he understand Russian, he understood that I was speaking Russian *to him*. He understood it as a distinct form of communication. If I withdrew it at this point, we would lose something special that had grown up between us. There wasn't, it felt like, any going back.

And yet at the same time this was happening, Raffi was going through one of his periodic bouts of bad behavior. They tended at this point to come in cycles. A month of good behavior followed by two months of bad behavior, of willful disobedience and tantrums. One of these started a couple of months before his third birthday. It involved running away from Emily and me when we were out for a walk—sometimes entire blocks away—in part because it got a rise out of us. It involved a certain amount of hitting. And it definitely involved taking a deliberately long time to do things like choose clothes, put on shoes, or head out the door—in other words, it was a kind of civil or sometimes uncivil disobedience against leaving the house.

I learned during this period that in Russian I was shorter tempered. I had fewer words and I ran out of them faster. I found I had a register in Russian that I don't in English, wherein I made my voice deep and threatening and told Raffi that if he didn't right away choose which shirt he was going to wear that morning, I was going to choose it for him. When he ran away down the street, I found myself without any embarrassment yelling in a very scary manner that if he didn't come back right now, he was going to get a time-out. (There is no Russian word for "time-out," so it sounded like this: *"RAFIK, YESLI TY NEMEDLENNO NE VERNESHYA, U TEBYA BUDET OCHEN' DLINNY* TIME-OUT!") I turned out to be more of a yeller in Russian than I was in English. Raffi seemed sometimes afraid of me. I

KEITH GESSEN

didn't want him to be afraid of me. At the same time, I didn't want him running out into the street and getting hit by a car.

Sometimes I worried about this; I still worry about it. Instead of an articulate, ironic, permissive American father, Raffi is getting a mushy, sometimes yelly Russian father with a limited vocabulary. It's a trade-off. I had a permissive mother and a strict father, and I was very happy. But they both had excellent Russian.

AT ONE POINT, I conducted an experiment. I had noticed that Raffi could instantaneously translate most Russian words, even fairly complicated ones, into English. But he refused to speak. Why? In my experiment, I said a common word—*lozhka*—and asked him to translate. "Spoon," he said right away. Then I held up a fork. "What's this?" I asked. "Fork," he said. "In Russian," I said. He earnestly tried and couldn't do it. The word, *vilka*, was certainly there—but in a part of the brain that he could access only in order to find the English equivalent. He hadn't built the neural pathways that would allow him to retrieve the word and speak it in Russian. He had zero practice, because he had zero need.

As I write this, I foresee a time in the not too distant future when what I need to say to Raffi, and the speed with which I need to say it, will be such that I'll have to switch to English. Even now (Raffi just turned six) I find myself doing it sometimes if we're having an argument and I need to make 100 percent sure he understands me. I think often of Werner Leopold's journal entry, late in volume 4, about taking a hike with a teenage Hildegard in the woods. It is 1944; Germany has been at war with the rest of Europe for half a decade; that magical visit to Leopold's family, when Hildegard learned to speak so well, is now in the distant past. Leopold continues speaking German to her, and she now answers, again, in English. On this walk, Leopold thinks of insisting that she speak German but decides against it; she is a teenager, and it's hard enough to get her to talk. "There is danger that much of what has been built up laboriously over the years will be lost," he writes, of her German. "But there are things in the life of a family which are even more important than the preservation of a linguistic skill."

There are things in the life of a family which are even more important than the preservation of a linguistic skill. For me and Raffi, I think, that is going to mean switching entirely to English one day, and reconstructing our relationship in that language (this language). And yet the seed will have been planted, I hope; should he wish to take up Russian again, he will have some basis on which to do so.

One of my fondest memories of our shared Russian happened when he was almost three, and I took him to a kids' singalong in a bar in Williamsburg. A Russian parent had booked the space, bought a bunch of bagels, and hired a singer, a woman named Zhenya Lopatnik, to perform some children's songs.

It was a memorable trip, just me and Raffi and a bunch of

Russian-speaking parents with our two- and three-year-old kids, eating bagels and singing along to old Russian children's songs whose words we only partly remembered. This group of parents was a lot like me. Most of us were more comfortable in English than in Russian; very few of us, I think, had any wish to go back to Russia. Why, then, were we doing this? What exactly did we want to pass on to our kids? Certainly nothing about Russia as it is currently constituted; very little about Russia historically. Yet somehow we could not let go.

Lopatnik sang several children's songs that Raffi and I did not yet know. Raffi listened politely. Then she sang Crocodile Gena's sad birthday song, and Raffi grew excited and did a little dance.

At the end of the kids' program, Lopatnik announced that she wanted to do some songs for the parents. "What do you think of Tsoi?" she asked. Tsoi was a songwriter and the lead singer of Kino, one of the greatest Russian rock bands. The adults cheered. She sang a song from Kino. Then she sang a famous though less cool Nautilus Pompilius song—"I Want to Be with You." The conceit is that the singer's lover has died in a fire and he longs for her, though in later years the author would insist that he believed the song had religious connotations and that the addressee was God. "I cut these fingers because they could not touch you," the song goes.

I looked at those faces and could not forgive
That they didn't see you and yet they could live.

We had never listened to this song together, and yet Raffi was transfixed. All of us were transfixed. The original Nautilus Pompilius version was accompanied by a lot of late Soviet-rock nonsense, like synthesizers and a sax solo. Stripped of these, in Lopatnik's rendition, it was a haunting song. "But I still want to be with you," went the refrain. "I want to be with you. I so want to be with you."

In that room, at that moment, it seemed not to be about religion but, as Nabokov said of *Lolita*, about culture, about language—about our longing to remain somehow connected to Russia, to Russian, despite everything. And the impossibility in so many ways of doing so.

Raffi hummed the Nautilus Pompilius song on the way home. A few days later I heard him singing it to himself as he played with some LEGOs.

Ya hochu byt' s toboy
Ya hochu byt' s toboy
Ya hochu byt' s toboy

And a few days after that, he said his first Russian sentence. "*Ya gippopotam,*" he said. I am a hippopotamus.

I was deeply, stupidly, indescribably moved. What had I done? How could I not have done it? What a brilliant, stubborn, adorable child. My son. I hope he never goes to Russia. I know that eventually he will.

Love and Anger

When your baby is born, you think you are a certain kind of person and are going to be a certain kind of parent. It's all a fantasy. You don't know anything about yourself until your baby gets older. You don't know anything about yourself until the day your adorable little boy looks you in the eye, notices that your face is right up close to him, and punches you in the nose.

The first two years were *physical*: breast milk and poop and Raffi's delicate little head that could so easily bump into something. Lack of sleep, of course. Worries that he would choke on something. But we survived. He hit his head a few times, but not too badly; one time he put a giant dead cockroach in his mouth, but I pulled it out and flushed it down the toilet.

And then he was two: He was running around, and wearing a little hat, and now we had to prevent him from getting hit by a car. He was a loud and rambunctious boy. He liked jumping up and down in his crib, or on our bed, or on one of us, if we made the mistake of lying down. One time my father was visiting and Raffi wanted to show off, so for half an hour he ran in rapid circles around our small living room yelling, "I am fire tuck! I am fire tuck!" He got kicked out of day care for refusing to nap and for jumping up and down on his cot, causing the other children not to nap. Someone around this time told us that the hard part was just beginning. We couldn't believe it. Harder than no sleep? Harder than waking up every ten minutes to google an imaginary symptom? Yes. Raffi had never been placid or well-behaved. But this was different. He now seemed to know what he was doing when he disobeyed us, and this made it so much worse. The advice books call it "testing boundaries." That didn't really capture the experience. Testing boundaries was your co-worker sending emails on the weekend. This was your coworker, when you picked him up, starting to scratch you. You turned him around so that he couldn't do that, and he reared his head back and headbutted you. He'd start swinging his little feet and some-times would catch you in the balls. There was frustration involved but also actual physical pain. He'd throw his milk bottle at you and it would hit you in the head.

Sometimes we tried to reason with him; other times we gave him a time-out, putting him in his room and locking the door for a few minutes. But he would come back out a few minutes later and just do whatever had gotten him in trouble again. Then he would get another time-out. He noticed the time-outs and didn't like them, but they didn't seem to affect his behavior very much.

I found the episodes of hitting and scratching very upsetting. There was the pain—that was part of it. But there was also the feeling of betrayal. Our little baby boy, whom we had fed and clothed and cuddled! Was this how he repaid us? Something else as well—fear. Was this our kid; was this what he was like? Had we done something wrong as parents that was causing this? Was it too late to correct course? All these thoughts and fears mixed together in moments of conflict and came forth, for me, as outrage. One time, when Emily was already quite pregnant with Raffi's little brother, we had a conflict over dinner. Raffi didn't want to eat his. He demanded a totally different dinner. Emily was inclined to let him have it. I disagreed. We had already run the bath, for one thing, and for another it was a perfectly fine dinner. After some back-and-forth, Raffi picked up my glass of water and doused me with it.

What the fuck! I tore off my wet shirt, picked up Raffi, stripped him of his clothes, and jammed him into the warm bath. He was terrified and bawling. I felt out of control. Emily was scared. She went into the bathroom to comfort Raffi while I stewed in the living room and gradually started to feel remorseful. Eventually I went to apologize. Emily urged Raffi to accept my apology. Raffi was reluctant. "Dada's not nice," said Raffi. And it was true: it was turning out that Dada was not nice.

Then came Ilya. Raffi, who was now just past three, did not resent his little brother, as far as we could tell. He did not throw tantrums or demand extra attention. But he did find him fascinating. He wanted to play with him. He wanted to grab his face and pull on it. He wanted to twist his head in ways it could not be twisted. He wanted to sit on his little brother and see what that was like.

One time when Ilya was just a few weeks old, I was sitting on the couch and holding him in my lap when Raffi came up and started trying to grab his head. "Stop that," I said. But he kept doing it—reaching in to grab the baby's head and try to pull it. Ilya, like Raffi, had been born at home, but he had then come down with a virus and we'd had to spend a miserable week at the hospital while they pumped him full of antibiotics. We had just come home, and I really needed Raffi to stop messing with him. But he wouldn't stop. So as I held Ilya with one hand, with my other I reached out to push Raffi away. I missed, or Raffi was moving, and instead of gently nudging his chest, my hand ended up kind of slapping the top of Raffi's head. He staggered back a bit and then called out, "Mama! Dada hit me!"

"Is that true?" said Emily, emerging from the kitchen. "Did you hit him?"

"Kind of," I said.

A similar incident took place just a few weeks later. We were at my father's house, and Ilya, now two months old, was on the carpet, trying to learn how to hold up his head. I was right there with him when Raffi came over and grabbed his face in both hands and started shaking him. "Stop that," I said. Raffi ignored me. "Stop that!" I said more forcefully, and still he ignored me. Finally I slapped his wrist. It was just his wrist, but I slapped it hard. "Ahh!" cried Raffi and ran downstairs to fetch his mother. "Dada hit me," I could hear him say.

These were the low points. But scarier to me were the times when Raffi drove me so out of my mind with anger that I would imagine hitting him for real. If I just gave him one smack, I thought, he would understand. He would leave his brother alone; he would leave his mother alone. He would stop being so violent. I felt this possibility inside me. I was capable of doing it. But I knew it was a bad idea. So instead I would yell and hector and reprove. I wanted some kind of acknowledgment from him that he was being unreasonable. But he was too little to give it to me. So instead he would just freeze up and stare into space and wait for it to be over. After each of these explosions I was so miserable. But I didn't know how to make it stop or what else to do.

"Dada's not nice." The words cut me to the quick. If there was one thing I aspired to be, it was nice. I wanted to be nice. I wanted my son to feel that I was a warm presence in his life. I wanted this now especially, when after Ilya was born I became Raffi's primary caretaker. Emily was busy keeping Ilya alive. I could keep an eye on Raffi. I was finding it very hard.

Near our place we had two playgrounds—a rich one and a poor one. The rich playground was well-kept, shaded by old-growth trees, and surrounded by beautiful converted carriage houses. The poor playground, next to a public housing project and a police station, was a little worn down and parched. In both playgrounds I saw good parenting, patient dads, attentive moms. And in both playgrounds I saw lousy parenting. One time on the poor playground a little boy of about three came up to me, crying, because he had scraped his knee. It wasn't a terrible scrape, but it was bleeding, and I said, "Let's get some water on that." I walked with the boy toward the water fountain. His father intercepted us. "What are you doing?" he said to the boy. "Stop complaining. Go back and play." The father didn't say anything to me, and I didn't say anything to him. The boy was his son. His son was going out into a tough world. He would probably be fine without putting any water on his cut. But, man—really? I went back to Raffi and we continued playing.

At the rich playground a few weeks later, I witnessed a different scene. It was late in the day and Raffi and I were one of the last father-and-son couples out there. A little boy, maybe six months younger than Raffi, was playing with a ball. Raffi, as was his wont, ran over to him and grabbed it. The boy started crying. I watched to see what would happen: usually when Raffi grabbed someone's ball, it was an invitation to run around and chase each other, an invitation to play. And that, in a sense, is how the action was interpreted by the little boy's father, who was wearing well-fitting shorts, a polo, and Ray-Bans. "Go get the ball!" he told his son. But he did not say it in a playful manner. He barked it like an order. "You want the ball, go get it." The boy was confused. He did not chase Raffi. The father was disgusted. "Let's go home," he said to the boy. I then caught

Raffi and got the ball from him and brought it back to the father. "Here you go," I said. He did not answer.

And I thought, Well, at least I'm not like that. But I also thought: Raffi is going to go out into the world filled with boys raised by fathers like these. Both were training their sons to be aggressive. The poor father wanted his son to toughen up and not complain. The rich father wanted his son to learn to take whatever he wanted. And I, too, by blowing my top too often, by not controlling my emotions, was teaching Raffi aggression, though not in any systematic or deliberate way.

THE MOST DIFFICULT TIMES were the early mornings and the late evenings. Raffi was always the first one up in our home: around six A.M. we would be startled awake by him noisily climbing into our bed and demanding that we bring him some milk. Emily would have been up several times during the night to feed the baby, so she needed more sleep. Sometimes I needed more sleep, too, and I would give Raffi my phone and let him watch the PBS Kids app until seven; but most times, because I thought the little screen would rot his brain, I would get up and take him out with me into the living room. Then the battle would begin to keep him out of our bedroom: what he wanted was his mother. She had less time for him now; she breastfed Ilya; poor Raffi was stuck with his grumpy Russian-speaking father. We had locks on the inside and outside of the kids' room, and on the inside of our bedroom, but not on the outside, so he would constantly try to sneak in there—most often when I was going to the bathroom. I would then have to go after him and drag him out, sometimes kicking and screaming and yelling for Mama. It wasn't the best way to start our days.

The midmornings also, I'll admit, when it was time to get out the door, were not great. Raffi was capable of getting dressed by now, but a lot of the time he didn't want to. He would run from me if I brought out clothes. Once dressed, he would suddenly become fascinated by a book or a toy that, twenty minutes earlier, could not hold his attention. Sometimes I'd be in a hurry because I had to get to work, but most of the time I just wanted to get on with my day. If it was up to Raffi we would simply never make it to day care. So here, too, I would find myself yelling or hissing or reprimanding.

Then he was in day care, during which time we would think only kind thoughts of him, and look at photos of him on our phones, and I in my mind would promise I'd never yell at him again. Then he'd get home and we'd start all over again. He didn't like his dinner. He refused to go to sleep. He made noises and tried to wake Ilya, whose sleep at the time was as precious to us as anything.

A friend recommended a book: *The Kazdin Method for Parenting the Defiant Child: With No Pills, No Therapy, No Contest of Wills*. It was by Alan E. Kazdin, PhD, a psychology professor at Yale and director of the Yale Parenting Center and Child Conduct Clinic. Kazdin had the answers; better than answers, he had *data*. At his parenting center he had seen thousands of children and their parents. He had tested his hypotheses. He knew how to fix what was wrong. I read the book on my phone with fascination in between bouts with Raffi and took screenshots of the best parts to text to Emily.

Kazdin is a behaviorist. This means he puts an emphasis not on relations, hierarchies, and needs, but on reinforcement. To support a behavior, you pay attention to it; to "extinguish" a behavior, you ignore it. Everything we'd been doing was wrong: the time-outs, the yelling, the belief that if we told Raffi to stop doing something enough times, he would actually, like a normal person, stop. And yet weirdly I was not discouraged to learn this. We'd been doing everything wrong but now we would do everything right: we just had to do the *exact opposite* of what we were doing.

Kazdin was a bracing read. Early in the book is a passage on what he calls "the punishment trap." "It goes like this," he writes.

Your child does something genuinely annoying or bad: hits his sister, breaks a lamp, or just screams and whines. You punish him for it, and he stops instantly. The experience of the punishment making the behavior go away has a profound effect on you. Next time this misbehavior occurs, you're more likely to respond with punishment. And there will be a next time. A great deal of scientific evidence shows that the unwanted behavior temporarily stopped by punishment usually returns at the same rate in the hours or days to come. All the punishment did was stop the behavior for a moment—which isn't bad, but you probably felt you had accomplished something more than that. As a child adapts to the punishment, the unwanted behavior tends to return faster.

Kazdin sums up: "Punishing a behavior is still a form of paying attention to it, and *any* kind of attention can encourage your child to do something again." In order for the punishment to have the same effect as before, you have to increase its severity. And then again, and again, as you become further ensnared in the punishment trap.

This was true to my experience. The first few times I'd yell at Raffi about something, he'd stop doing it. Then he'd start doing it again. So naturally I yelled louder. The behavior did not improve.

In *The New Basics*, Michel Cohen advises time-outs, and I used them liberally—too liberally. They had long ago ceased to be effective. Kazdin knows all about this. "Speaking of time-outs," he writes, "plenty of experts explain that you give a child a time-out so that he can think about how he got into trouble. This is a complete misunderstanding of time-out, which is not about thinking at all. We know this because animal research proves that time-out works with all sorts of mammals that do not have our cognitive power. In a time-out, we simply withdraw attention for a brief period."

Ah! I thought. "A complete misunderstanding of time-out,"

as proved by animals! Raffi was an animal; I was an animal; Emily was an animal; Ilya was a baby animal.

I loved the book: I loved its certainty, its practicality, its lack of mumbo jumbo. I finished it one cold winter day while Raffi was napping. I couldn't wait for him to wake up and face his new, scientifically informed dad.

The method part of the Kazdin Method is all about reinforcing good behavior. Kazdin calls it "catching them being good." He advises looking for good behavior and then lavishing praise on it. As for bad behavior, he advises ignoring it. You should also work on anticipating possible problems and heading them off with some kind of incentive, he says: for example, rather than spending all your time in the store fighting over whether Raffi will get a piece of candy before finally breaking down and giving it to him, why not tell him he'll get a piece of candy if he behaves himself well in the store? He gets the same piece of candy, but now you get something too. For slightly older kids, Kazdin says, you can build a sticker chart, tracking their progress around various behaviors and giving them stickers that will build up to an eventual reward (a slice of pizza with Dad; a trip to the dollar store to get a new toy). I told Emily about my new discoveries, and though she found them philosophically revolting—like we were going to give Raffi a quarterly performance review at the corporate job that was his childhood—she agreed that we could try.

Some of it worked. Going to the store became easier, and some other small journeys, given a clear objective and clear reward, went more smoothly. But some of it did not work. Dinner-time had always been a problem. Raffi just didn't want to sit with us and eat. He would start to act out. One night, fresh off my reading of the Kazdin book, we were ready. Raffi threw his food onto the floor and we ignored it. He went over to the coffee table and threw the books onto the floor; we ignored it. We also ignored his running into the kitchen and turning the recycle bins upside down; dumping the shoes from the shoe rack onto the floor (again); chasing Swizzle with a sneaker in his hand. Finally, unable to get our attention, he ran at Emily with his fists in the air, ready to strike her in the stomach, for fun. She put up her hand to defend herself and caught him with her fingernail on his cheek. Immediately he started bawling. "Mama!" he said. "You scratched me!"

And so it went for weeks. We would ignore him and ignore him as he marauded around the house, and then finally he'd do something—hit the baby, draw on the wall, or (a favorite of his, and for some reason especially infuriating to me) start spraying the baby's milk bottle all over the apartment—and we'd yell at him. Finally he'd calm down, having gotten what he wanted (our undivided attention), but we would feel terrible and defeated. Maybe if we'd managed to ride out the storm a few times to the end, he'd have stopped behaving that way. Or maybe we would have ignored him until he'd found a knife and cut himself with it. I don't know. In any case, we never managed.

(We even, in a fit of desperation, built a sticker chart for him. Emily drew the icons: he would get a sticker for eating his dinner, for not hitting anyone, for getting dressed in the morning in a timely fashion. Raffi, to our surprise, did not find the sticker chart offensive, but he did insist that we also have sticker charts, and when we asked him what should be on ours, he proposed the same stuff: we'd get stickers for not hitting him, for eating our dinner, and for getting dressed. We put all three sticker charts on the fridge and kept up with them for a few days. Emily and I got the maximum number of stickers—we ate our dinners, put on our clothes, and didn't hit Raffi. Raffi's record was a bit more mixed, but he didn't seem to care. The idea of building up a number of stickers toward a grand total of stickers was beyond him. [To be fair, Kazdin recommended four as a start age for this method, and Raffi was about three and a half.] Raffi was happy as long as we got stickers on our charts, and he was allowed to put them on there. The fact that he wasn't getting many stickers on his chart didn't bother him at all. We abandoned the experiment.)

The worst part of it was that Raffi by now was not oblivious to the fact that I was constantly mad at him. The things he'd say about it were really sad. "Dada," he said once, "superheroes never get mad." Around the same time: "Dada, I love you even when you do something bad to me." (By this he meant turning off the TV or reproving him.) One night I spent two hours trying to get him to go to sleep. We had developed a not-great system in which I'd lie next to his little toddler bed while he drifted off. Recently this had become an invitation for him to roll over onto me, or reach out and pinch my cheek, or kick me.

Eventually I'd lose my patience and tell him I was leaving and do so, locking the door behind me. He would then bang on the door with all his might. Since I feared this would wake Ilya, I would relent and come in and plead with him to be quiet. He'd agree and lie down, and I'd lie down also, and then after a few minutes he'd start rolling and pinching and kicking again. I'd leave again, and we'd start it all over. Somehow I thought that eventually he would grow tired of doing this, and eventually he would in fact lie down and go to sleep. But it was always a struggle and there would be various points at which I'd very, very quietly (so as not to wake the baby) yell at him. On one such night around this lousy time (he was about three years and eight months), he said, "You're a bad dada and I'm never going to listen to you again!" I felt he was right. I was not a good dada. But I didn't know what else to do.

THIS WAS THE AGE at which Emily's ideas about parenting and mine most seriously diverged. Emily thought I was too strict, a yeller. I thought she was too permissive. The biggest arguments turned out to be about TV. Emily thought it made sense to hand Raffi a phone and let him watch a show on the PBS Kids app if we were on the subway, or eating out, and he was tired or cranky. I thought this was the road to ruin: to Raffi expecting and demanding the phone in every possible situation. I think we both had a point. But in practice it was hard to meet in between. When we were together, one of us would win and the other would resent it; when one of us had Raffi on our own, we basically had two different sets of rules.

This was also the age at which we really started wondering whether Raffi was more badly behaved than other kids. Screaming infant Raffi, non-napping toddler Raffi, tiny destroyer-of-our-apartment Raffi could all plausibly have been phases. But now we began to wonder if this was it, if this was him. And how much of it was our fault?

I watched our friends who had kids our age. None of them had perfect angels. Some of the parents were better at anticipating the needs and moods of their kids than we were; some of them got mad less quickly than I did. But ultimately it was our kids who determined how we behaved. The parents of Raffi's best preschool friend, A., were a lot like us, alternately yelling, threatening, cajoling, because A. was a lot like Raffi: a high-spirited and occasionally violent little boy. Whereas our friends Matt and Emma, the parents of Raffi's other best friend, E., were a lot more chill, because E. was a lot more chill. The parents had a role to play—Matt and Emma had always been chill, as far as I could tell, and that had rubbed off on E.—but ultimately it was the kid who set the tone. And Raffi set a very particular tone.

We had a terrible trip to Bareburger. We knew it was a bad idea to go there, but we didn't know how bad. Once we got seated, Raffi dropped his crayons onto the floor. Then he started playing with the salt. Then his water. He spilled his water all over the table. We cleaned it up. The food came. Raffi chewed on his hot dog for a minute and then threw the rest of his meal to the floor.

When a child is in a situation in which he is behaving horribly, you should take him out of the situation. I knew that much. So I grabbed Raffi and carried him out of the restaurant. As I did so he hit me in the face and clawed at me. He was a little guy, but it still hurt. I tried, without dropping him, to get his hands farther from my face. By the time we were outside I was holding him upside down and shaking him so he would stop. He went from crying and whining to laughing. But it wasn't a happy laughter, like when we wrestled on the bed or he had told a poop joke that he liked. It sounded to me like a desperate laughter. I was holding him upside down and I was angry—and he was scared. His response to being scared in this instance was to laugh. I put him down. Emily came out of the restaurant with Ilya. We drove home miserable.

We had a terrible trip to the playground with A. and his mom. Raffi and A. liked to wrestle with and hit each other, and A. definitely gave as good as he got. Once a week we'd get an email from the preschool with the subject heading "Scratch." Raffi was playing with a "friend," the email would say—because all the kids were referred to as "friends"—when they had a disagreement, and the friend scratched Raffi. Then there'd be a photo of Raffi's face with a scratch on it. Sometimes a quite deep one! When he got home or at pickup we'd ask Raffi who had scratched him. "A.," he would say matter-of-factly. "Why did he do that?" we would say. "Because I hitted him." "Why did you do that?" "Because he scratched me." And so on. I'm sure A.'s parents also got emails about stuff that Raffi had done to A. We didn't talk about it.

So I was prepared for a little bit of roughhousing at the playground. But it turned out that the instigator was Raffi. He kept coming up to A. and trying to knock him down or pull his shirt or just hit him for no reason. I found it embarrassing. I ran over and pulled Raffi off A. I told him to stop. The second time it happened I told him that if it happened again we'd leave. I repeated this threat the third and fourth time it happened. The fifth time I finally had to carry it out, even though I didn't want to, because if you threaten consequences, you have to deliver on them. Even the lax discipline books agreed on that. Raffi wailed and howled. I felt horrible. That night I told Emily what had happened. "Oh, that's exactly what happened last week when we went with A. to the playground." "Raffi kept hitting him?" "Yes. And I told him that if he didn't stop, we'd have to leave, and he didn't stop, so I had to take him home." I was shocked. In this one instance, we'd done everything right, had been totally consistent from one situation and parent to the next—and it hadn't mattered.

Throughout all this, he could also be adorable. He loved dancing and making up silly names. For a while he loved singing "Twist and Shout," which he referred to as "Shake It Up, Baby," and which I'm pretty sure he thought referred to an actual baby. He liked running around naked and he also liked hiding under things, towels or blankets or recycle bins, and popping out eventually and saying "Here I am!" It would almost have been easier to deal with his misbehavior if it didn't alternate so consistently with moments of warmth, cuddliness, generosity ("Dada, here is a cozy blanket that you can borrow from me"), and unbelievable cuteness. I wanted to grab him by his thin little shoulders (he never ate anything) and yell, "Act like this! Act like this all the time!"

IN RETROSPECT I CAN see that I was being too tough on him. Not for hitting A., necessarily, but in so many other, smaller ways. I pushed him too hard. There was a period of time when he stopped wanting to walk up the stairs to our apartment. He would reach the vestibule downstairs, declare himself tired, and plop down onto the floor. It was two long flights of stairs to the third floor, but in just about every instance he had spent the entire walk home running away from me, or jumping into piles of snow, or just generally being a maniac. Clearly he could walk up the stairs, and I thought it was important that he do so. I would say, "I'll see you upstairs," and go up to our apartment, and eventually, most of the time, he would join me. And in retrospect this was fine, I guess, except that when Ilya, three years later, started doing the exact same thing, in a different apartment, with fewer stairs, I decided not to have that battle with him. I would just pick him up and carry him up the stairs.

At the time, though, I kept reading books. I read and found useful Adele Faber and Elaine Mazlish's book *How to Talk So*

Kids Will Listen and How to Listen So Kids Will Talk. The basic idea is that you need to try to enter the child's perspective. If Raffi suddenly announced that he did not like mac and cheese (although he did), or worse, that he did not like his school friend A. (although he definitely did!), my automatic reaction was to contradict him, to set him straight. This was a mistake. What you should do, and what I did manage to start doing here and there, is accept the premise. "So you don't like mac and cheese? When you see mac and cheese you want to throw it out? You would rather eat grass?" Something like that. His experimental hatred of mac and cheese now having been indulged, Raffi would some of the time go ahead and eat his mac and cheese.

I read and found useful a book called *Love and Anger: The Parental Dilemma* by Nancy Samalin, based on a series of parenting workshops that Samalin hosted in the 1980s. The book consists of parents talking about what drives them crazy about their children and then the horrible things they do or (mostly) say in their anger, and then recounts the ways they try to improve. Some of the things the parents say are truly harsh, way beyond anything it would ever occur to me to say to Raffi. "It served you right," one mom confesses to yelling at her bawling seven-year-old after throwing all his favorite toys down the trash chute because he failed once again to clean them up. "Now, go to your room. I don't even want to see you for the rest of the evening." Jeez, I would think. I'm not a monster like these people; I don't need this book. Then something would happen with Raffi, and I would return to it again. Some of the advice was helpful, but I found especially encouraging the descriptions that parents gave of what drove them nuts. One father speaks of his son's "dawdling" as being the thing that gives him the most trouble, and this seemed very true to me. And I loved the word. That's what Raffi did every morning when I was trying to get him out the door—not active resistance, not sabotage, but dawdling! From then on, whenever he did it I would think of that other dad, how he hated dawdling, and grow a tiny bit less annoyed.

And it was a primarily descriptive rather than prescriptive book that finally helped me (and Raffi) survive this year of our lives. It was called *Your Three-Year-Old: Friend or Enemy*, and its authors, Louise Bates Ames, PhD, and Frances L. Ilg, MD, were, like Kazdin, from Yale; they were associates of the pioneering developmental psychologist Arnold Gesell, who, back in the 1930s, started studying children as they went through their stages of development. Ames and Ilg's book is comparatively old (they were most prominent as commentators on children's development in the 1950s), and what they propose is not so much a method, like Kazdin's, as a series of observations. The authors spent decades watching the behavior of little kids (through mirrored glass, I always imagined), and in their patient and generous way they describe it all: the aggressiveness, the sudden mood swings, the stubbornness about every little thing. Ames and Ilg, following Gesell, believe that little kids develop in approximately six-month cycles—a cycle of relative calm and happiness at two and three is followed by storm clouds at two and a half and three and a half. This did not track exactly with our experience, but it was pretty close. There really had been periods of calm with Raffi. We had taken them to be simple maturation: this is what he'd be like from here on out. But then he'd revert, or get worse in a new way. Ames and Ilg were here to explain it.

"Three is a conforming age," they write. "Three and a half is just the opposite."

> Refusing to obey is perhaps the key aspect of this turbulent, troubled period in the life of the young child. It sometimes seems to his mother that his main concern is to strengthen his will, and he strengthens this will by going against whatever is demanded of him by that still most important person in his life, his mother.

This was right. It was antiquated a little, and the next paragraph describes the mother doing things (taking the child to school, to the bathroom, getting him ready for bed) that, in our family, I did, especially after the baby was born. But still, for all my troubles with Raffi, and these increased in proportion to the amount of time I spent with him, it was Emily who bore the brunt of it. It was Emily who was at the center of Raffi's universe; it was Emily to whom he gravitated. The articulation of this truth, reaching through clear time to the muddy present, was immensely helpful.

And there was something else in there as well: the empathetic description of the child as going through a turbulent and troubled period. This was new to me, this idea of Raffi not as a problem to be solved, but as a person going through difficulty, a little person but a person still.

There was much more along these lines. The book has practical advice—anticipate battles over getting dressed and eating and try to head them off by lowering the temperature—and it has some charmingly old-fashioned formulations: "Most Three-year-olds eat well enough alone in the kitchen, with their mother near at hand." (Ames and Ilg capitalize the "Three.") "Some can manage, without incident, at the family table. However, for some the family situation is too complex and they are likely to be too demanding of attention and their dawdling, poor table manners and food refusal are apt to get them into trouble, especially with Father." Watch out for Father! (Although this one too rang true. I tended to be the one who got most upset when Raffi poured salt on the table or threw his food onto the floor.) But the things that really amazed me were the descriptions of his inner life:

> Parents sometimes fear that their Three-and-a-half-year-old is deaf when he so often disregards what is being said to him. Surprisingly, he may respond best when whispered to. Actually, the child of this age may have many auditory fears. He is afraid of the banging of the radiator, the sound of a siren, the noise of thunder. He may even fear or be made uncomfortable by the sound of a loud voice.

Poor little guy! This riotous, hard to control, occasionally aggressive little boy was also scared of loud noises. He certainly heard a loud voice often enough in our home—mine. Poor little guy.

And again, in a passage about late toilet training, a perceptive remark about his relationship with his mother:

> But with others this lateness of training and inability or even refusal to function may be part of the life-and-death struggle that some are carrying on with their mothers.

Yes, I nearly yelled as I read this: yes. Raffi did not want to kill me and marry Emily. It was more complicated and more difficult than that. What he wanted was all her attention even as he also wanted to be his own person. He wanted to re-create the relationship they'd once had, when he was smaller, but in a way that it could no longer be re-created. He wanted the impossible and he knew it and it drove him crazy. It almost literally tore him to pieces. It really was life and death, though mostly it was life, the heartbreak of life.

So I read this book. I read it slowly, with immense gratitude, and here and there I was able to make some adjustments. It was so helpful to know that what Raffi was doing was normal, or, let's say, within the range of normal; that he couldn't help himself; and above all, that it would pass. I found, at night, that if he was acting up it wouldn't do to try to restrain him. I could not lie on top of him and make him see reason. Instead, if he wanted to fight, I would curl up into a ball and cover my head and let him wail on me. He wasn't very strong. Eventually he'd get bored and lie down in bed and let me read to him.

But more than anything, as Ames and Ilg also predicted, time passed. Raffi changed and we got one of our periodic reprieves. As he approached four, he was still willful, sometimes violent, and reluctant to go to sleep, but his main activity shifted from defying us to explaining to us the world. I was keeping a diary of incidents in which I'd lost my temper, and at a certain point the diary shifted over to cute little things he'd said.

This morning [he] woke up and smiled at me. "Dada, I had a dream that we went to the museum together. There were crocodiles."

"Dada, I actually like you! When I was little I didn't like you."

In the garden: "When stink bugs hear the noise of a big scary thing walking"—makes himself into a big scary thing—"they roll up into a ball."

At dinner: "Dada, these fish used to be real but now they are dead and we can eat them."

"Dada, look, I'm going to eat one of them, see?"

Has become interested in death: "Do we sleep in the ground after we are died?"

"Dada, is our world safe?"

Asks if "after dinner" (breakfast) he can have ice cream from the fridge. I say we'll have to ask Mama. "Yeah, after she wakes up." Then: "Dada, if *you* would like to eat some ice cream you can go to the deli that's very close to our house."

"Dada, a date and a prune are a kind of big, big, big raisin. Dada!"

Arranges a bunch of keys on the floor. "Hey, Mama, do you like the collection I made?" "Yes, that is a beautiful collection." Raffi, shrugging: "These are just keys."

Laying down the law: "No shoes in the kitchen!"

More death: "Dada, what if you and Mama die and then the baby and I get old and we cry without you?"

There were still many terrible bedtimes and too-early mornings during this period. There were still blowups. I still lost my temper. He still harassed his little brother. But one could see an end to it, or at least a pause. It would not last forever, or not in this exact form.

I remember a weekend morning around this time, when Raffi was approaching his fourth birthday. He got up late for him, at seven, and came into our bed. I had been up with Ilya since 5:30 and had just put him down for a nap and was hoping to snooze for a bit. Raffi demanded milk. I fetched it and then lay down between him and Emily and closed my eyes. Sometimes Raffi liked to doze off again after his milk, or just take a while to drink it. Even five more minutes would be something. But Raffi finished the milk, threw the cup at me, and then from where he lay elbowed me in the nose.

I hated getting hit in the nose! It was so painful and embarrassing. I grabbed Raffi and carried him screaming and crying into the living room. I couldn't lock him in his room because the baby was asleep in there. I couldn't lock him out of our room because he'd bang on the door and wake up Emily. I knew from Kazdin that time-outs don't work, but Kazdin himself admits that sometimes parents just want justice. Raffi had hit me in the face for no reason and I wanted justice. I headed for the bathroom, put him down in there, and shut the door.

"No," cried Raffi, almost to himself, "not again!" I don't know where he'd picked up that expression, but he had taken to saying it a lot. A few days earlier, I had given him five frozen blueberries and he'd thrown them onto the floor because he wanted more than five. We discussed it and I told him that he could only have five. He agreed, but when I once again gave him five, he cried, "Oh no, not again!"

So here he'd said it, even though I had never before locked

him in the bathroom. It sounded so pathetic. And in fact the reason we never locked him in the bathroom was that there was too much stuff in the bathroom he could mess with. I didn't trust him in there, and that, more than anything, is why I opened the door and went in and sat down on the toilet.

He was crying inconsolably.

"What's going on?" I asked.

"I want Mama!" he wailed.

I looked at him, at my little boy. He was a lot like me and he was a lot like his mother. I thought of his complex inner life, the one that Ames and Ilg had told me all about. I thought of all the things he feared and wanted and didn't understand.

"I'm not Mama," I said. "But I'm Dada. Come here."

He let me hug him until he stopped crying, and then I, in turn, let him watch some TV. It wasn't over, this battle between us. It would, maybe, never be over. But here we were.

Picture Books

In Raffi's half bedroom there was a large white, cushioned high-backed chair that we had inherited from one of Emily's friends. It had stood for a time in our living room, but Swizzle scratched it up very badly, and by the time Raffi came along we were glad to move it somewhere else. For the first three years of Raffi's life, we sat in that armchair, in his half bedroom, and read him books.

We began reading to him at what felt like a ridiculously early age, when he first started to be able to focus his gaze. He was a captive audience: he didn't even know how to crawl. Our first book was *Pat the Bunny* by Dorothy Kunhardt. "Here are Paul and Judy," it begins. "They can do lots of things. You can do lots of things, too." It wasn't really a book so much as a series of little activities. But also it was a book. I hated it and admired it. It was from 1940. Nothing had come along to supplant it. More than seventy years later they were still printing thousands of copies. It could not have been a simple process: the book includes inside it a mini-book ("Judy's Book"), as well as a tiny mirror and a patch of fake rabbit fur. All this for $5.99. At first

Raffi merely stared at the pictures, but eventually he started patting the rabbit fur and putting his finger through "Mummy's ring." Soon he started tugging on and ripping the book. By the time it was his brother's turn, we had to get a new copy.

It's possible we were imagining it, but Raffi seemed to really respond to books. He loved being scared by them; he loved the little songs that some of them elicited from us; at the end of *The Very Hungry Caterpillar*, when the hungry caterpillar turns into a beautiful butterfly, he always said, from the earliest age, "Ahhh."

I loved discovering this new world of books alongside Raffi. I had never read the English-language books, nor had them read to me. It was like we were traveling into this land together. And I found myself having strong reactions. When you read a book once, you develop some opinions. When you read a book a hundred times, you develop *very strong* opinions. I was delighted, and surprised, by Maurice Sendak's *Where the Wild Things Are*: a magical book, worthy of all the praise. I was disappointed by *The Very Hungry Caterpillar*: Eric Carle, its author, was a magnificent illustrator, but words had always meant more to me than pictures, and I found Carle's prose awkward. I loved the Frances books by Russell and Lillian Hoban, came to have a grudging admiration for the Knuffle Bunny books by Mo Willems, and was lukewarm toward the Harold and the Purple Crayon books. *Dragons Love Tacos* I threw into the trash. Among the Russians, I loved Chukovsky, Kharms, and Vladimir Suteev, and was disappointed by Samuil Marshak, Agniya

Barto, and Vladimir Mayakovsky. Some books grew in stature with repeated readings—Sendak's *In the Night Kitchen*, on first reading a work inferior to *Where the Wild Things Are*, eventually won me over with the richness of its illustrations and the wackiness of the ominous little songs the bakers sing. *That's Not My Penguin*, meanwhile, began to seem stale, and also debris started sticking to its fuzzy cover. *The Gruffalo* and *Click, Clack, Moo* could both be read a hundred times with pleasure. And as for *Goodnight Moon*, by Margaret Wise Brown: I loved *Goodnight Moon*. It is genuine poetry, as Brown's biographer, Leonard S. Marcus, would later write: "accessible but not predictable, emotional but purged of sentiment, vivid but so spare that every word felt necessary." I thought it was a haunting and beautiful book, and I was willing to read it as many times as Raffi asked.

There were books I could not read because I would start crying. When you are reading to yourself, you can cry and keep reading; when you are reading aloud, it's much harder. For the first year of Raffi's life I found I could not read *The Runaway Bunny*, also by Margaret Wise Brown. The book is about a little bunny who threatens to run away; his mother tells him that if he runs away, she will run after him—"for you are my little bunny." The bunny does not give up. "If you run after me," he says, "I will become a fish in a trout stream and I will swim away from you." "If you become a fish in a trout stream," says his mother, "I will become a fisherman and I will fish for you." The book's next image, in full color, covers two pages and shows the bunny in the water and his mother with a fishing rod, reaching out to him. "If you become a fisherman," says the bunny, "I will become a rock on the mountain, high above you." "If you become a rock on the mountain high above me," says his mother, "I will become a mountain climber, and I will climb to where you are."

Reading this aloud instead of silently; reading it aloud to a little person who didn't totally understand it; reading about the passionate love of a mother for a little person just like him . . . I never got past "mountain climber." The publisher's description assured me that children would be "profoundly comforted by this lovingly steadfast mother who finds her child every time." Maybe—I can't speak for Raffi. To me the book seemed like an expression of terror and madness: the mother's terror of losing her child and the madness this caused in her. Emily had that madness, and so did I. We couldn't let Raffi out of our sight. We worried about him all the time. Car rides, as I've said, when he just screamed unceasingly from the back seat, were torture. Sometimes Emily climbed back there to keep him company. One time during that first summer, while we were stuck in traffic on Canal Street, I turned to them from the driver's seat and saw that Emily was crying too. Raffi had stopped screaming and fallen asleep. "What's up?" I asked.

"I don't know," she said, crying. "He's just so precious."

And he was. I felt the same way. The idea of anything happening to him was intolerable. No book captured that feeling as well as The Runaway Bunny. It was too much for me.

———

OF THE WRITERS WE REGULARLY read, the only one whose biography I knew was Kharms, and that was because he is famous as something other than a children's writer. Perhaps the reason I didn't know anything about the others was that they were boring—artists and writers who had chosen a relatively lucrative career and then lived happily ever after.

My first clue that this was not the case came while sitting in that big white chair in Raffi's room and reading Eric Carle's *From Head to Toe* for the hundredth time. I noticed, on the copyright page, a strange dedication. "For Herr Krauss," it read, "who introduced me to modern art even though it was forbidden." This was puzzling. Why did Herr Krauss have a German honorific, and who was forbidding him to show modern art? I looked it up on my phone after Raffi had gone to bed. Carle, it turned out, had been born in Syracuse, New York, in 1929 to a German émigré couple who later became homesick and returned to Germany, Nazi Germany, in the mid-1930s. This was about the same time that Werner Leopold was taking his daughter, Hildegard, back for a visit. But the Leopolds had no thought of staying! The Carles, incredibly, did. A few years later, Germany started invading its neighbors, Eric's father was drafted into the army, and off he went to the eastern front. He was eventually taken prisoner by the Soviets and then, as was common with German prisoners of war, kept on in a labor battalion after the war as a form of reparations. Carle himself, then a teenager, was forced to dig trenches on the western front. But before that, one of his high school art teachers, Herr Krauss, had introduced him to the work of Klee, Matisse, and Picasso, and that was the meaning of the dedication. After the war, Carle left Germany and returned to the United States.

This biography explained so much: Carle's slightly tin ear came from his not having grown up speaking English; his transcendent belief in the power of colorful collages came from his exposure, at a critical time, to Matisse and Klee; and the basic innocence of his books, the absence of any threat or hint of violence, may have been a defensive psychological reaction to the trauma of the war. His near contemporary Sendak, who was safely in Brooklyn throughout the fighting and the murder, was nonetheless touched by the Holocaust—family relatives from Poland perished, and Sendak said the event hung over his adolescence and extinguished any belief he may have had in God. The Hitler moustaches on the bakers who try to put Mickey in an oven in the night kitchen were not a slip of the pen. For Carle, who saw men blown to pieces by Allied air power, a Sendak-like reference to the war would have been much harder to pull off. In short, he never touched it. I can think of no major American picture book oeuvre that is more innocent.

After this minor discovery, I became fascinated with the biographies of the writers in Raffi's room. Seuss, for whom my respect had been waning, turned out to be a real piece of work, a multimillionaire who drove his loyal wife to suicide by having an affair when they were in their sixties. Sendak was prickly, eccentric, and gay, a man with a chip on his shoulder because neither the art world nor the literary world took him entirely seriously. And then there was Margaret Wise Brown, unlucky in love but lucky with her biographer, Marcus, whose book *Margaret Wise Brown: Awakened by the Moon* locates Brown at the very center of the maelstrom of modernism. You could see this for yourself easily enough in the illustrations of her books by Clement Hurd and Leonard Weisgard, but what I hadn't known about was Brown's roots in the progressive schooling movement of the 1920s and '30s. She had been part of a writers' workshop at the experimental Bank Street School in New York City, specifically devoted to creating a children's literature along Deweyan principles of experiential learning. The Bank Street literary philosophy was a rebellion against innocence, cuteness, and the countryside, in favor of realism and the big city. Brown turned out to be the workshop's most talented alumnus: her wonderful *Noisy Book* is her most programmatic Bank Street work, though some element of the everyday (mixed with magic) remained a hallmark of all her books. And yet she, like Sendak after her, was never accepted as a serious writer in her own lifetime, and was even rejected by the New York Public Library's main children's book buyer, Anne Carroll Moore, for her heretical Bank Street stance against the fairy tale.

The Russian children's writers had, as usual, more turbulent lives. Kharms, dead of starvation in a mental hospital; his friend Alexander Vvedensky, whose small book about two brothers who go on a Crimean vacation Raffi and I read together, dead of pleurisy on a prison ship at the age of thirty-seven. Marshak barely escaped arrest. So, it turned out, had our beloved Chukovsky. He had been a successful literary critic and magazine editor before the revolution, had stayed on in Russia after 1917 despite the evident danger, had written most of his great children's poems in a burst of creativity in the mid-1920s, and had then been hounded into silence by the country's librarians, led by Lenin's widow, Nadezhda Krupskaya, who thought his inspired but silly rhyming poems were no basis on which to educate the future socialist youth. He was forced to recant and was eventually rescued only by the reestablishment of a more conservative aesthetic under Stalin. But he was done by then as a writer of children's books. He lost his youngest daughter, Mura, to tuberculosis when she was eleven—this happened not long after his recantation, and he would believe to the end of his long life that her sickness and death were a punishment for his cowardice. His other daughter, the wonderful novelist and memoirist Lydia Chukovskaya, lost her husband to the purges in 1937. Chukovsky's youngest son perished fighting the Nazis. Chukovsky lived long enough to see himself become a Soviet institution, to provide shelter for Solzhenitsyn when he was being hounded by the KGB, and also to see his other son, a successful novelist in his own right, bring shame to the family by signing a letter denouncing Boris Pasternak's Nobel Prize. Chukovsky describes (sometimes elliptically) these twists and turns in his fortunes in a remarkable diary that was published long after his death and that is one of the great documents of twentieth-century Russian literary culture. So that was the author of all those stories about talking hippos.

But it was an American writer whose biography I found most disturbing: Russell Hoban, author of the Frances books, of all the books in our library the ones that most prominently featured parents. Parents are usually absent from children's books. The mother in *Where the Wild Things Are* calls Max a "wild thing" and sends him off to bed without his supper—but she is never seen. The parents in *In the Night Kitchen* are "sleeping tight" while Mickey falls down past them to the night kitchen, and so too are the parents in Chukovsky's *Barmaley* when Tanya and Vanya sneak off to Africa. The mother in *The Cat in the Hat* infamously leaves her children alone all day in the charge of a nervous fish! The point of these books is to create a world where children are on their own, having an adventure, possibly being in danger, before returning safely to bed or their rooms or Leningrad, in the end.

The six Frances books, published between 1960 and 1970, were an exception. They are about a small badger named Frances who is very clever and very rebellious. In these books, Frances's parents, also badgers, not only play a significant role, but are terrific parents. They are patient and funny and they come up with creative solutions for Frances's problems. When, in *Bread and Jam for Frances*, Frances refuses to eat anything but bread and jam, they start giving her bread and jam at every meal, until finally she breaks down in tears and asks for spaghetti and meatballs. ("I had no idea you liked spaghetti and meatballs!" says her mother, triumphant.) When, in *Bedtime for Frances*, she refuses to go to sleep, they indulge her to a point, and threaten a spanking when she goes too far.

The books are written in a lapidary style somewhere between poetry and prose. They do not rhyme or have a discernible rhythm, but they have deliberate line breaks and a strong sense of how the text will sound when read aloud. The first lines of *Bedtime for Frances*, for example, are as imprinted on my brain as any lines of poetry I have ever read. "The big hand of the clock is at 12," the book begins.

The little hand is at 7.
It is seven o'clock.
It is bedtime for Frances.

If I was reading these lines, it meant that Raffi was on his way to sleep—not without a struggle, to be sure, not without some drama, but on his way regardless. And the book would help. It was, in that sense, incantatory.

The first Frances book is illustrated by Garth Williams, most famous as the illustrator of *Stuart Little*; the rest by Hoban's wife, Lillian. When they began to be published, the books marked a watershed for the depiction of family life in picture books. "Family life was fair game," writes Barbara Bader in her exhaustive history of the American picture book, "and of those who pursued it none were more successful than the Hobans." The writer Bruce Handy, in his book on children's literature, declares that Frances's parents "may well be the best mother and father in all of literature." They really do seem to be wonderful, and it's not crazy to think, as you read the books, that

Russell and Lillian Hoban, like Frances's parents, knew what they were doing.

So imagine my surprise when I read up on Russell Hoban. He was born in Philadelphia in 1925 to a Jewish family from Ukraine. His father was a socialist who worked for *The Jewish Daily Forward*. Hoban went off to fight in the war at eighteen, saw combat in Europe, returned, and started working in advertising and also as an illustrator and occasional author for magazines, including *Time* and *Sports Illustrated* (he did a striking portrait and write-up of Floyd Patterson for *SI* after Patterson became world heavyweight champion in 1956). He and Lillian had four kids, three of them girls. They moved to Connecticut and made the Frances books together. And then in the late 1960s, Hoban went through what he later described as a "midlife crisis," moved the family to London, and declared that he wanted to stay. Lillian took the four kids back to the States. The couple divorced. And Hoban stopped writing the Frances books and started instead writing novels for adults.

I found this information deeply disturbing. It was not just that the perfect family depicted implicitly in the Frances books was not perfect, but that Hoban seemed to have turned his back on Frances. One of the novels he wrote shortly after the breakup with Lillian includes a disaffected children's author who says she doesn't have "another furry-animal picnic or birthday party in me." It was hard to read this as anything but a dig at *A Birthday for Frances* and *A Best Friend for Frances*, two of the later (but still excellent) Frances books. What the hell! I listened to a recording of an event with Hoban in London from 2010, a year before his death. It was filled with fans of his most famous novel, the postapocalyptic *Riddley Walker*. During the Q&A, Hoban was asked how he was able to spend so many years writing novels with limited commercial prospects, and his answer was that he had once, long ago, written some successful children's books that still brought him an income. That was the only mention during the event of the Frances series. I felt like I was listening to a man who had escaped an old life, changed his identity, and lived a whole new life—and was getting away with it. I felt indignant.

I walked around for a few months feeling this way. Russell Hoban—divorced. Frances's dad—a home-wrecker. Frances herself—abandoned. If those adorable little badgers couldn't make it, what hope was there for the rest of us?

READING THE PICTURE BOOKS, you could see why one of the great works of formalist literary criticism—Vladimir Propp's *Morphology of the Folktale*, from 1928—uses children's stories as material. They have a limited number of plots: A child (or childlike animal) goes on an adventure, finds himself in danger, and then, either because he is clever or brave or because he is rescued, escapes. There is a crisis, and it is resolved. The bunny in *Goodnight Moon* does not want to fall asleep, which is why he is taking so long to say goodbye to everything in the room, and why the old lady is saying "hush" to him. But he does eventually fall asleep. Night falls. Everyone rests.

I found the stories to be a form of communication with little Raffi. There was so much about the world that he could not understand. In her attack on Chukovsky, Krupskaya, reading too literally, had chided him for failing to come up with models for socialist behavior. In his defense of his own work, and of the fairy tale more generally, Chukovsky stressed his craft: what children needed was good poetry that engaged their imaginations. The rest would follow. At around the same time, in the U.S., Bank Street was arguing, against the fairy tale, that it was vital for children to recognize their own experiences and surroundings in the stories they were reading. I think both Chukovsky and the Bank Street writers were right, and the best of their stories combined talking animals and real-life problems. The runaway bunny is a talking bunny; Dr. Aybolit flies in an airplane to save Tanya and Vanya from Barmaley. For Raffi, it didn't matter if animals talked in the stories; he knew from life with our obstreperous cat that real animals do not talk. But it was interesting to consider the things they might say if they did talk, or what life would be like if they walked among us, making conversation.

Most of the stories have happy endings. Frances eats her spaghetti and meatballs; a crocodile eats (and then regurgitates) Barmaley; the moon man returns to his shimmering seat in space. (A nice exception was Marshak's poem "The Silly Mouse," in which a little mouse complains petulantly about all the animals who read him bedtime stories, until his desperate mother invites a cat to do so, and the cat eats the little mouse.) The purpose of the books is on the one hand to draw you in; on the other to lull you to sleep. Many of them employ rhythmic formulae and repetition. The best of them can approximate the sounds of ocean waves lapping against the shore.

We read in wild streaks—two weeks of this, a week of that, and then they'd be banished for months, only to return again. For a while we read *The Owl and the Pussycat* by Edward Lear, which we had in an edition with lush illustrations by Jan Brett. Raffi liked it so much that he demanded I recite it to him multiple times even after the lights were off. So there was a period of time where I lay on the bed next to his crib, held his hand, and did a song version of the poem. Then Raffi tired of it and we moved on.

I was amazed—and dismayed—by the gap in the quality of Russian versus American picture books. There were half a dozen great Russian children's writers over the course of the twentieth century; there were maybe ten times that many in the U.S. The emigration that had so enriched American intellectual life was evident as well in picture books. Eric Carle, Tomi Ungerer, Esphyr Slobodkina. And then there were the publishers. Russian books were cheaply printed and often crudely illustrated, whereas an American publisher had had the wit to ask Jan Brett to illustrate an 1871 poem by Edward Lear. Capitalism! There were many things wrong with it. But it had created the incentives for a children's book explosion like none that had ever taken place.

It would be nice to think that we sat in that white chair, Raffi curled up in our laps, and forgot all our problems. But the world followed us everywhere. I found the Knuffle Bunny books particularly upsetting in this regard. Trixie and her parents live on two floors of a brownstone in a very nice neighborhood that Brooklyn readers will recognize as Park Slope—so why do they have to go out and do their laundry? (Most brownstones have laundry in the basement.) And why so little laundry? And why, if they are going from one place in Park Slope to another place in Park Slope, past a third place in Park Slope (the school)—why do they go through Prospect Park? It is not on the way! Is the author of *Knuffle Bunny* merely reminding us that he lives near a beautiful park, in majestic Park Slope, and not, for example, near a Superfund site in Gowanus? Or above a bar on Franklin Avenue? Nonetheless, we read the book, and its sequel, to Raffi, because they were good books, and he loved them.

EVENTUALLY, I HAD TO move on. Ilya became old enough to be read to, and it fell to me to do it. Emily kept reading to Raffi, while I went back to the beginning: *Pat the Bunny, The Very Hungry Caterpillar, Goodnight Moon*. It was different the second time around, and in many ways better: I knew about more books, and more books had been published. In addition to my favorites from the Raffi years, we read *Moon Man* and *Not Now, Bernard*, and then *King Baby, Grumpy Monkey*, and *The Snurtch*. During my period of being mad at Russell Hoban, I had bought all the Frances books, even the very last of them, *A Bargain for Frances*, in which Frances has to trick her clever friend Thelma into giving her a china tea set (she sings: "Mother told me to be careful / But Thelma better be bewareful"), and manages to do so, thereby in effect *ending* the series, because Frances has become, if not her parents, then at least someone who has absorbed much of her parents' genius. Perhaps the Hobans' marriage, like the Frances series, had run its course. In any case, Ilya and I read these books over and over again. They were such good books.

Occasionally it would happen that Raffi listened in. He would claim not to want to, that he was too big for these books, that he had read them as a baby, but almost always he would stick around, and lay his head on my shoulder, and start elbowing Ilya out of the way. "Stop that, Raffi!" Ilya would say, and sometimes hit Raffi or scratch him or pull his hair, and then I'd have to stop reading and separate them, and sometimes we managed to get back to the book, though not if one of them was crying.

Raffi's books became longer and more complicated. Emily and he went through every Captain Underpants and Dog Man, then Roald Dahl, Beverly Cleary, the Moomintroll books, and Harry Potter. Even the best of them were less like poetry and more like novels. They had fewer and fewer pictures until, with Harry Potter, they had no pictures at all. Meanwhile Raffi grew bigger and bigger, and when he lay in our bed, he took up more and more space.

I would get to those books eventually, I figured, with Ilya. I wasn't, I now found, in any hurry.

A School for Raffi

In the middle of our most difficult year, the year that Ilya was born and Raffi was a three-year-old terrorist, the year of Kazdin and *How to Talk So Kids Will Listen* and Ames and Ilg, we were tasked by the City of New York with finding Raffi a proper school.

We had been thinking about this moment, and preparing for it in our way, and dreading it since . . . I was going to say since the day he was born, but that would not be true. On the day he was born, and we were alone with a tiny creature that barely knew how to open its eyes—on that day our choice of Raffi's school seemed very far away. And once we got out of the terrifying miasma of his infancy, the thing we needed to find was not a school but a day care. Asia was not forever. It took us a while to find Ms. D., who ran a small day care out of the ground floor of her brownstone, but when we did find her, we were very happy. We had cleared a major parenting hurdle. For a few weeks we didn't need to think about anything. Then we started thinking about schools.

It occurred to me as we did so that I'd hardly ever noticed

these large redbrick buildings that took up entire blocks. Why should I have? You could not buy a coffee in them, or a beer, or borrow a book—they were just massive buildings that one had to endure on walks through the city. I had no idea what was going on inside them, and I didn't care. For years, I had done a lot of my writing work at a Starbucks on Seventh Avenue in Park Slope. There was a great chicken kebab place across the way from it, and on the next block a pretty good pizza place, which would later make an appearance in Noah Baumbach's *Marriage Story*. And across the street from the pizza place, *not* featured in *Marriage Story*, there was some kind of school. I laugh at the thought now, at my ignorance. "Some kind of school." That was PS 321! It is the largest and most famous of the Park Slope elementary schools. It is by some accounts the best elementary school in Brooklyn.

Once I began to see the schools, I could not unsee them. I realized how much of life was organized around them. Wealthy homeowners had the resources and the motivation to put time and money into their neighborhood schools; good neighborhood schools in turn attracted other wealthy homeowners. Studies of adjacent neighborhoods had repeatedly shown that a slight increase in test scores in the school zoned for one neighborhood would increase property values in that neighborhood, with various cascading effects. In New York, where school zones were drawn seemingly at random, sometimes even running down the middle of a street, no parent would buy or even rent a home without first figuring out what school it was zoned for. These inauspicious brick buildings, hiding behind their anonymizing PS numbers, held the key, apparently, to lifelong happiness and success.

But there was, in addition to test scores, something else. The very week that Raffi turned one, the journalist Nikole Hannah-Jones published a cover story for *The New York Times Magazine* called "Choosing a School for My Daughter in a Segregated City." The piece is the culmination of a decade and a half of reporting on education, first for a local paper in North Carolina, then for ProPublica and eventually the *Times*. During that time, Hannah-Jones discovered not only that American schools were not integrating but that many were actually resegregating. School districts in the South that had been under court-ordered integration mandates had either had their mandates lifted or the mandates had stopped being enforced. According to Hannah-Jones, the high-water mark of school desegregation in the United States came not recently, or semi-recently, but in 1988! The reasons for this were manifold and complex, but they came down to white parents not wanting to send their kids to schools with Black children. And in almost no big city was the problem worse than in New York—that is the segregated city in the headline of Hannah-Jones's article about her daughter.

Segregated schools led, as the Supreme Court had ruled in 1954, to unequal educational experiences. Resources follow white parents. There were PTAs for elementary schools in the city that raised a million dollars a year. There were other PTAs that raised a hundred dollars. These monies paid for music teachers, auditoriums, outdoor gardens. Schools with these kinds of resources were almost like private schools, in a sea of less fortunate schools. In New York, they were almost all majority white.

And how could this happen in a city as diverse as New York? Well, it wasn't *that* diverse, actually, on a neighborhood level: areas of central Brooklyn that had already undergone gentrification, like Park Slope, were now mostly white. Areas that had not been gentrified were still mostly Black. But in areas that remained, at least for the moment, racially mixed, like the part of Bedford-Stuyvesant where we lived, middle-class families (both Black and white) tended to find ways of getting their kids into majority-white schools. They might enroll them in a magnet school that did not care where they lived, or a Gifted and Talented Program,* or a charter school. They might lobby the administration of a desirable nonzoned school to let them in. Or they might move.

Hannah-Jones's articles depict a tragedy in which individuals who meant well conspired with those who did not to enforce

---

*Not long after Raffi was born, I met a fellow journalist whose four-year-old had recently taken the Gifted and Talented test. "It's really unfair," said the journalist. "You can hire an expensive tutor who will prepare your kid. All the test does is test how much you've prepared." "Incredible," I said. "But you didn't do that, right?" "No, we did," said the journalist. "The tutor was very nice and he had these games he played with our son that prepared him for the test." The boy had aced the test and secured admission to one of the city's most sought-after public schools. But, my colleague went on, there was a kind of darkly comic denouement: the boy missed his tutor. "After he took the test, he asked us why his 'friend' wasn't coming anymore."

segregation. In her *New York Times* piece, she describes the story of PS 8 in Brooklyn Heights, which was for years a mostly Black and Hispanic school with low test scores, neglected by well-off parents in the neighborhood who opted to send their kids to private schools. In the mid-aughts, through the concerted efforts of a multiracial group of parents to secure more funding and raise the school's profile, the school began to improve. This attracted more well-off, largely white families, who were able to bring even more resources to the school. Eventually this second generation of school gentrifiers started pushing the Black students out. They took over the PTA, especially the fundraising, and started seeking to separate their children from other children: Why should their kids be in class with a child who had serious behavioral issues, for example, because he lived in a homeless shelter or because he had seen violence in his home? Gradually those students and their parents began to feel less welcome at PS 8.

One of the most depressing things in the article is a quote from Kenneth Clark, a pioneering Black social psychologist whose work on the self-image of Black children underpinned the Supreme Court's decision in *Brown v. Board of Education*. Clark himself, Hannah-Jones points out, moved from Harlem to Westchester so his kids could go to school in an affluent, majority-white district. "My children have only one life," he said. And this, Hannah-Jones argues, is the problem with our country. Everyone, or at least a lot of people, had nice values, in theory. But when push came to shove, they did what they thought was best for their kids. As one Brooklyn parent tells Hannah-Jones, "My kid's not an experiment."

I couldn't get the article out of my mind. I, too, obviously wanted what was best for Raffi. But if what was best for Raffi was not best for another child, if it came at that other child's expense—was that worth it? Would it be something that Raffi himself would want? A few months after the article came out, I got Hannah-Jones to come to my university to talk about her work. Chatting before the event, we learned that we lived pretty close to each other in Bed-Stuy. I told her that as a journalist I worked mostly on Russia, and she was surprised that I was interested in her articles.

"I'm a Russian who lives in America," I said, by way of explanation.

Hannah-Jones smiled. "You're a Russian who lives in Bed-Stuy," she said.

Indeed I was.

A few weeks later, in November 2016, a white supremacist was elected to the presidency of the United States. The diversity numbers in some of the elementary schools in Brooklyn began to seem not just problematic but monstrous. PS 321, in Park Slope, had 3 percent Black kids; PS 107, also in Park Slope (the school featured in *Knuffle Bunny Too*), also had 3 percent Black kids. In Brooklyn? In 2016? It was disgraceful. The more I thought about it, the more I was convinced we needed to do things differently. Hannah-Jones cites research showing that the only way to improve our schools and narrow the achievement gap between white and Black students is integration. Good old integration. We were white, which meant that we should attend a school where whites were in the minority. In Brooklyn, in Bed-Stuy, that would seem to have been easy enough. But then we toured the schools, and it turned out to be a lot more complicated than that.

THE FIRST TOUR WE TOOK was at our zoned school. This school was not considered a top school. Its test scores were well below the city average. But it had a nice building, with colorful murals out front, and a cute cafeteria where we picked up our community-supported agriculture (CSA) vegetables. It was near our house. And it was, on paper, diverse—15 percent of the students were white, 16 percent were Hispanic, and 65 percent were Black. Sixty-five percent of students qualified for free or reduced-priced lunch. That looked like Brooklyn to me.

The tour took place in December. A group of about thirty parents, some of whom we recognized from the neighborhood, packed into a small classroom and listened for an hour as the (white) principal talked about his philosophy for the school. When he explained that the students followed a "Leader in Me" program, based on the *7 Habits of Highly Effective People* self-help book, the room grew tense. This was not what these Brooklyn parents wanted to hear. We wanted to hear about play-based learning, stacking wood blocks, sharing a communal experience. When the principal said that later grades followed the "active learning" Teachers College curriculum, the parents calmed down. Or anyway, I calmed down. That sounded fine. The principal also said that the school's pretty sad playground was going to get an upgrade soon from the School Construction Authority. So far, so good. Then he admitted that the school did not have enough pre-K seats for all zoned applicants. That was a surprise.

It got worse. The principal did not take us into any classrooms, but we happened to see some as he took us on a tour of the building. When I had seen the diversity numbers—65 percent Black, 15 percent white—I imagined that each classroom had roughly that proportion of students. But what I saw in the school was something different. The older classes were predominantly Black and Hispanic. And the younger grades—pre-K in particular—were predominantly white. The parents in the tour were almost all white too. Raffi would be attending a nominally diverse school, but he would actually be in a majority-white class. And we might not even get in!

The next school we toured was just a few blocks west, but it was very different. Its test scores were the best in the district. They were not Park Slope level, but they were close, and unlike in Park Slope, the school's racial makeup was mixed—14 percent white students, 75 percent Black and Hispanic students. Thirty-nine percent of the students qualified for free or reduced-priced lunch. The tour I went on confirmed these numbers and much else. Rather than thirty white parents for the tour, there were about a hundred racially diverse ones; rather than hosting us in a small, stuffy classroom, we were in the spacious school auditorium. The school was also doing some impressive fundraising. Rather than telling us about how they were hoping to get a new playground in the coming year, the parent coordinator told us that the PTA had a budget of half a million dollars. "But this school is not just for people who can show up and write a six-figure check," he said. "This school is for everyone." All I heard was "six-figure check." So some people did show up with six-figure checks.

But more than anything I was struck by how the school was genuinely diverse, throughout the grades. As far as I could tell, this was a deliberate decision on the part of the school's administration. The school clearly prided itself on being both integrated and successful: the leadership of the school was Black, but the students who helped with the tours were Black and white, as were the PTA representatives who led the tours. I knew from a few newspaper accounts and from some parents that the school was not a racial utopia, that there had been tension between the Black families who had been part of the school for years and the white families who were new to the neighborhood, but from where I sat it looked pretty good. I loved it, and as someone looking in from the outside at a school his child would probably not be able to attend, I hated it. It didn't seem fair. As one parent friend who'd also been on the previous tour, of our zoned school, put it to me: "I can't believe this school is four blocks away from that school." But so it was.

By this point I had started to hate my fellow white parents. Also myself. We listened to the principals and parent coordinators and nodded our heads in appreciation, occasionally asking ingratiating questions—"Is there room for parental involvement?"—to show how engaged we planned to be. (That was me, actually, on the tour for our zoned school.) We all looked the same and thought the same, and the only difference between us was whether we lived a few blocks north or a few blocks east— whether we were zoned for the school we were touring, or were not. (Also, whether we owned our housing, meaning, in this case, whether we could easily or sort of easily move.) How did we have time for all this? Didn't we have jobs? And other children? Why did we think it was so important that our child go to the best and most wonderful school? It was normal for us to go on the tours, to see what the schools were like, but it was also messed up. Schools should not be subject to consumer demand. You should get your school assignment and go to that school! If that were the case, if that were the system, then parents who had time enough to go on seven tours would also have time to make sure that *all* the schools were good, since they didn't know which school they'd end up at. (This was the basis of Rawlsian liberalism, and it was a good one.) But that was not the world we lived in. It was especially not the world we middle-class, mostly white parents lived in. So we went on the tours.

Next I toured an old Brooklyn school that I'll call PS 1. Just as our zoned school was four blocks east of the more successful school I had just visited, PS 1 was four blocks east of our zoned school. It was in an old, handsome brick building that I had passed at least a hundred times while walking to and from the C train. But I had never been inside. PS 1, I now learned, was facing some difficulties. It had once had an enrollment of a thousand students; now it was under four hundred. A majority-Black school, it had been decimated by the gentrification that had taken place in our neighborhood, as old families were priced out and not replaced, at least not yet, by new families. On the very cold day in January when I visited, along with just four other parents, many of the pre-K students were missing. I asked the parent coordinator, who was leading our tour, why. "A lot of the parents live far away, or in shelters," she said. "When it's really cold out, it's just too much of a journey."

The other parents asked questions. "We used to have that" was the parent coordinator's answer to many of them—about one of the after-school programs, about some of the curricular offerings. They also used to have an active PTA, she said, but now the parents worked too many hours or lived too far away. The PTA could use some help, she said.

But at the same time, the school was beautiful and warm. The parent coordinator showed us a classroom for early drop-off; it was usually attended in the mornings by a volunteer, she said, or by the principal. It was impossible to imagine the ambitious principals of either of the other schools I'd visited doing free early morning childcare. We looked in on an art class, where the students huddled around the teacher as he showed them how to draw a bird. The principal herself was straightforward and honest and was fighting to keep her art and music teachers—those luxuries are the first to go when your enrollment starts dropping. (Next, you start losing classrooms, and they put a charter school in your building.) The building, a little run-down, remained majestic. A plaque inside the entrance read, TO THE BOYS OF P.S. [1] WHO DIED DURING THE WORLD WAR. I think the war in question was World War I. The school had a low PS number, and later I looked it up: it had been at that spot in Brooklyn since the middle of the eighteenth century.

So those were our choices: Our actual zoned school, appealing for its small size and proximity but in the grips of hypergentrification. The superior school a few blocks west, racially and economically diverse and run like a tight ship, but impossible for us to get into. And PS 1, where almost half the students were chronically absent, where entire classrooms sat unused because enrollment had dropped so dramatically, where there was really no telling how much of the school would remain intact three or four years from now. PS 1 was the just choice; the school to the west was intriguing but out of reach; our zoned school was the laziest choice, though in this case there was a virtue to laziness. But all the choices were imperfect.

There was, on top of all this, another twist. We were still living in our old apartment on a loud street above a bar. We had come to love the neighborhood; Raffi was friends with everyone on our block; and our enemy, the bar, had even gone out of business and been replaced by a much quieter and more respectful bar. But the rent kept going up; the arrival of Ilya had made the apartment seem pretty cramped; and Mr. O., our landlord, complained constantly (and not unjustly) about Raffi making too much noise above his head. We might be able to stay another year or two, but eventually we'd have to move. So whatever choice we made now regarding schools was subject to revision or even cancellation, depending on where we ended up. We began talking about moving so much that Raffi picked up on it and started saying that we needed to "tell the construction workers" (they were all over our neighborhood, building condos) what kind of house we wanted. Raffi wanted, he said, a front porch, to play on with his friends.

LOOKING BACK ON THAT time now, I see several things. One is my almost total lack of information. I didn't really know anything about the schools beyond what I saw on the tours and read in the very brief and often euphemistic write-ups on a site called Inside Schools.* I hadn't even noticed, for example, that the school to the west, which I so coveted, had uniforms, and that the kindergarten kids in the classrooms we visited were sitting quietly at their desks as the teachers ran them through their phonics. All I saw was that the kids were diverse and that the school had its act together. But more than that, I just didn't understand what a school *was*, what it did. I was looking at the schools as an adult and thinking of whether they served the

---

*Compared with a hack site like Great Schools, Inside Schools, a nonprofit run out of the New School, was a legitimate source, with up-to-date Department of Education data as well as reports of site visits and some narrative description. Still, it was hardly enough information on which to base a decision about where to send your child to school for the next seven years.

cause of social justice, as I understood it. I didn't and couldn't really see them from the perspective of a child.

The other thing I see now is my moral vanity. I alone, I thought, could see the gentrification in the schools; I alone could fix it. All the other white parents were racists; I was the lone anti-racist. I was going to be the one person who made the just choice.

The thing about moral vanity is that it does sometimes lead to justice. You have to believe that your individual choice is significant; that even if it seems to bring about no systemic change, it can make a difference. This is what Russian and Soviet dissidents have shown over and over again through the centuries—that one person doing the right thing can show others that they need not be afraid. There is moral vanity in that, if you like. But others who were more morally modest—the great children's book author Chukovsky being one example out of many—and who found a way to play along with the Soviet system even though in their hearts they opposed it, probably prolonged the existence of that system beyond its natural life span. Whereas the occasionally annoying, strident, self-congratulatory dissidents helped bring it down.

In my case, though, I think moral vanity led me to over-interpret my limited data. The school that most needed help was obviously PS 1. But I was wrong about our zoned school. Three years after I concluded that it was on the verge of being engulfed by gentrification and becoming practically all white, it hasn't been. White parents send their kids there for pre-K and

K—and then leave. One white neighbor recently admitted that he was worried about sending his own kid there because the older grades were all Black. He said he was ashamed to be thinking that way, but there it was. Hannah-Jones had been absolutely right.

I was not there to see this change, or non-change, because Raffi wasn't at our zoned school. As the deadline for the pre-K application approached, I had become increasingly obsessed with getting him into the school to the west. My parents had moved us from Russia to America so that we wouldn't have to endure the Soviet education system; surely I could figure out a way to get Raffi into a school that was just a few blocks away from us. One of our neighbors had transferred there from our zoned school; he said that it only took ten visits to the principal's office. But that was a lot of office visits. That was more office visits than I would be able to manage. So I came up with a different solution. As part of our search for a new apartment, I included the calculation that it would be nice—all other things being equal—if the apartment were zoned for the school to the west. And we eventually found one that was. It was in a brand-new building, with an elevator; it had two bathrooms; it was actually smaller than our old apartment, but it was better laid out, with a separate second bedroom for the kids. It was in a mixed-income building and you had to make less than a certain amount to qualify, but luckily we made less than that certain amount! "It's the first time that's worked in our favor," Emily commented. It felt like serendipity. There were some warning signs about the place—for example, the sidewalk leading up to it was closed for future construction, and across the street was another future construction site—but the construction hadn't yet started, perhaps the developer would go bankrupt and it would never start, and anyway we were told by the leasing office that the new construction would not rise all the way to our apartment, which was on the twenty-first floor. From our window we could see all of eastern Brooklyn. And finally, the address was zoned for the school we wanted Raffi to attend. We signed the lease, and the first person we told about it was the lady who answered the phone at the Department of Education. "We're moving," I said, and told her our new address. She put it in the system. A few weeks later, we got the letter from the DOE—we had received a spot at the school to the west.

My heart sank a little when I read the letter. It meant we were really moving, leaving the neighborhood that we loved so much, where so much had happened, where Raffi had spent the first four years of his life and both our kids had been born. And it seemed like we had made a compromise, though its exact outlines were unclear to me. For one thing, I had no idea whether Raffi would like the school, whether he would thrive there, whether it was the right place for him. At the same time, I felt like we had done, if not the right thing, then the rightish thing. We hadn't gone to rescue PS 1, but at least we hadn't abetted hyper-gentrification at our zoned school. We had pursued integration, but in a way that didn't inconvenience us very much. That seemed like an OK choice among three imperfect options.

Now I see we did the wrong thing. We moved to a place where we didn't actually want to live. By dipping into our limited but in this case sufficient savings to switch school zones, we arguably took a spot at the school from someone who needed it more. Most important, the things we brought to the school—some free time, a few hundred dollars a year in PTA contributions, our "advocacy"—were things the school already had, in far greater quantities, from other parents. I had read Hannah-Jones too literally, or self-servingly; her argument, though framed in terms of race, was more widely about sharing resources. That's not what we were doing by enrolling at our school.

On the other hand, by the time Raffi entered kindergarten, there was plenty of room for most people who wanted to go— by then we were in the middle of the pandemic, and the school was just looking for anyone willing to show up.

King Germ

On the last day of school, March 13, 2020, the last day of normal life, the last day before the plague officially hit New York, Emily and I got in the car and drove to Fairway.

It was, in some ways, a strange choice. Other people were already getting out of town or staying home so they could avoid contagion. We were going to stock up on cheese and coffee and pasta and vegetables at a high-end grocery store in Brooklyn.

For those who don't know, Fairway was and is an old Upper West Side grocer, a kind of proto–Whole Foods, with excellent produce and dairy products at reasonable prices that expanded into a mini-chain in New York and New Jersey in the early aughts. In fact, they overexpanded and went bankrupt, but at this point they still had the Red Hook location. It was right on the water and had a view of the Statue of Liberty, which Raffi when he was little called the Statue of Livery. After we bought our car, right after Ilya was born, we started going there every Sunday afternoon to shop for the week. The kids usually fell asleep in the car on the way, and then while Emily shopped I would stay in the car with the sleeping children and read or write some emails. If the kids woke up, I'd take them for a walk along the water or to the cafeteria in the back of the store. So maybe it wasn't such a strange place for us to go when the world was ending.

On our way to Fairway, I thought about disaster. I had spent so many years watching disaster movies—*War of the Worlds*, *World War Z*, *The Day After Tomorrow*. I was no prepper, just a red-blooded Russian-American who wanted to be ready when the time came. Now it was here. I was ably steering our car down busy Atlantic Avenue.

It was odd for us to be out together like this without our kids. It felt a little like we were on a date, though in other ways it did not feel like a date at all. We passed the Trader Joe's on Court Street. A long line of people stood on the street waiting to get in. We resolved not to do that to ourselves at Fairway; if there was a line, or the parking lot was overflowing, or people were fighting over shopping carts, we would leave.

But Fairway was calm. There were parking spaces. No carts were available, but people were coming out with them; I waited a minute while an older couple unloaded theirs and inherited it. I was resourceful! Then a woman, mistaking me for an employee, asked if she could have the cart. I said she could not, then felt bad about it. I was an asshole! But we, too, needed to do our shopping.

Inside the store, things were basically normal. There were no bananas or toilet paper, but there was soap and pasta. I hadn't come up with a pandemic shopping list and wasn't sure how to make myself useful. Emily bought what she usually bought and multiplied it by three. I remembered that a dad friend had told me the other day at school pickup that he'd procured a giant bag of rice. That seemed like as good an idea as any. I put a giant bag of rice in our shopping cart.

After we filled our cart, I stood in line for forty-five minutes while Emily went outside. In line I read Ludmilla Petrushevskaya's great short story "Hygiene" on my phone. I had it on my phone because I'd once translated it. It's a terrifying story about a rapidly spreading disease that ravages an entire family and everyone around it, sparing only a little girl and her cat. The men of the family reveal themselves to be violent idiots. The women aren't much better. Only the little girl behaves decently. The lesson of the story was to be nice to your family. The virus was going to do what it was going to do, and no amount of ingenuity or "hygiene" was going to change that. The only thing you could control was whether you'd suffer together or apart.

As usual, this was easier said than done. The family in "Hygiene," for all their troubles, has only one kid.

ONCE WE GOT HOME with our groceries, Emily went back out, into Manhattan, to do some publicity videos for her second novel, *Perfect Tunes*, which was to come out in mid-April. I put the groceries in the refrigerator and went to pick up the kids.

The last few months had actually been a pretty turbulent period in the life of Raffi. Pre-K, at first, had been magical: our school was everything we'd hoped it would be. Our teacher, Ms. V., was the perfect mixture of strictness and kindness, and at our first parent-teacher conference, she told us that Raffi wrote his sevens backward and didn't know what a rhombus was, but that otherwise he was a sociable and well-behaved young man. Then, a few months later, she started sending emails home to let us know that Raffi was making fun of G. and punching R. in the stomach. We had a meeting with her and came up with a plan. Ms. V., it turned out, had a background in behavior modification, so it was back to Kazdin and the star chart for us.

There were other storm clouds. Our new apartment not only had a separate bedroom for the kids but also soundproof floors, a dishwasher, and, as mentioned, an amazing view of Brooklyn; but the week after we moved in, the giant construction project across the street that I'd hoped would go bankrupt instead commenced. The noise was so loud that we could never open our windows; one time the noise was so bad that when I walked out of the building with Ilya, he burst into tears. We now lived much closer to Raffi's preschool friend A., he of the "scratch" emails, as well as another close preschool friend, J., who was so nearby that we could see his apartment from our window, but otherwise the neighborhood was unappealing and, though in our school's zone, pretty far from the actual school. Every morning was a struggle to get both kids out of the house early enough and every afternoon was a struggle to get them back home again. In the mornings, Raffi would sometimes refuse to get dressed, and in the afternoons, he would refuse to leave the playground.

Sometimes I had to drag him from there, kicking and screaming. One time a passerby somewhat judgmentally commented on this as I was dragging him down the street by his armpits. She said, "You lost a shoe." Raffi had literally dug in his heels, and his shoe had fallen off. I let go of him and went to fetch it.

As we were meeting with Ms. V. about the star chart, extracting Raffi from the playground, wondering if our new apartment was a place we wanted to stay, we began reading about the strange new virus in China. We read about how it was spreading rapidly in Italy. We read about the first cases in the United States. We knew that the disease seemed to spare children; somehow we didn't think it was coming to New York.

Now it was here. All that week, that last week, they'd been talking about it at school. Ms. V. taught the kids to get through an entire rendition of "Happy Birthday" while they washed their hands; their dance teacher taught them to sneeze into the crooks of their elbows. I explained what I could about it to Raffi; because I did so in Russian, and because *corona* in Russian as in many other languages means "crown," Raffi had translated "coronavirus" as "King Germ." We found this very charming. In the news and on social media we followed with rapt attention the debate over school closure. The teachers' union and some members of the city council were calling for schools to shut down; the mayor was resisting. The situation was in flux—every day brought a different interpretation of what was happening and different predictions for the future.

After returning from our trip to Fairway, I walked to Raffi's school. When I got there, it looked no different from any other day: it was full of people and everyone was smiling and it seemed like such a success. It was a success. Raffi's after-school teachers were, as usual, exhausted. I told them I'd heard the mayor on the radio that morning saying that he wasn't going to close the schools.

"They have to close," one of the teachers said. "Attendance is already down. If he doesn't close them, we will."

That's when I knew the schools weren't opening up again.

We went to the playground so that Raffi could play with his friend M., as he always had. The playground was packed. Some of the parents seemed to be trying to keep their distance from one another; others not so much. As usual, it was a whole procedure to get Raffi to leave. Then we got Ilya, came home, and that was that. Two days later, on Sunday, the mayor announced in an anguished tone that the schools were closing. So were the day cares. The lockdown had begun.

IN RETROSPECT, WHAT WAS the worst part? All the different stages were pretty bad, though in different ways. For us, the lockdown itself, from roughly March 15, when the schools closed, to July 6, when camp opened, also took place in various stages.

The Sunday of the school closure, Emily and I both came down with sore throats. The next morning, I had a high fever and she had an even sorer throat. There was no way to get tested at that point, and neither of us had a cough, but still we decided to quarantine. For that entire first week, we stayed inside with the kids.

Our apartment was 877 square feet, and most of the space was taken up by the bathrooms. The bedrooms were small; the kitchen was part of the living room. Even by New York standards, for a family of four, this apartment was pretty cramped. The saving grace had been that it was an easy apartment to get out of: you took an elevator, walked through the lobby, and you were in the greatest city on earth. But we were not supposed to leave our apartment.

It was a long week. We watched out the window as traffic became increasingly sparse on Atlantic Avenue. On the first non-school day, we watched the athletic field down the street fill up with little kids and their parents, though you could see that the parents were keeping the kids from playing with one another. The construction site across from us was still going full tilt. It felt like the biggest change was that the schools had closed, and we were trapped in our apartment, and our kids were there too. We were too sick to do anything but turn on the TV for them, and that at first was OK. They watched an endless cycle of *Wild Kratts*, *The Cat in the Hat*, and the Netflix Captain Underpants show. Every time I got up the energy to turn off the TV, Raffi would say angrily, "Dada, why are you so serious? Don't always be so serious!" Most of the time that week, I just turned the TV on again.

The rest of the time I lay in bed and tried to figure out what to do once we recovered. As I read about the social distancing rules in San Francisco (no playdates and no playgrounds, they said, because kids are incapable of social distancing), I felt increasingly certain that we couldn't survive in our apartment, that we had to leave New York. But where would we go? My sibling, Masha, and their family had already driven up to Cape Cod and rented a house near my father. That seemed like a reasonable plan. I spent most of my nonfeverish hours that week looking at places near my dad on Airbnb.

We didn't end up going. Both of us had lived in New York for two decades and knew it as well as we knew any other place. When things got really bad, this was where we wanted to be. On top of that, we couldn't really afford to leave. Long before there was any talk of a global pandemic, I had taken a yearlong sabbatical from my teaching job, at half pay. The idea was that I'd make up for the loss of income by writing a book (in fact, the book you are reading). But I was not going to be writing anything if we had no childcare. Meanwhile, Emily's novel *Perfect Tunes*—a book about motherhood and art, about the impossibility of their coexistence, which she'd worked on for five years, through the birth of two children and our various moves and peregrinations—was due out soon. The week we were sick she had a call with her publishers; her book tour was canceled. There was some talk of pushing her book back to the summer or fall, but they decided against it. In short, while going to the Cape sounded nice, it was not necessarily a great time to take on another several thousand dollars' worth of rent.

A few days after we'd made up our minds to stay, I got a text from Eric, my old friend from grad school. He and Rachael and the kids had gone out to their place on Long Island, and he wondered if we'd like to house-sit for them in their three-story townhouse in Crown Heights. Their house was beautiful and had long been an object of envy to us; it also felt more hygienic than a crowded high-rise. As soon as we felt well enough to go, we packed our Fairway groceries, some clothes, and some toys, and moved to Crown Heights.

THAT FIRST WEEK, while we were still sick and trapped in our apartment, was bad. But once we recovered and moved house, things did not magically improve. Part of us thought that just having more space, more beauty, a backyard—all the things we had always lacked, living within our means in Brooklyn—that this in itself would solve our problems. It did not. Raffi now had his own room and a bed he claimed to like, but he still came into our bed at two A.M. every night. We now theoretically had an office with a desk that one of us could work in while the other watched the kids, but in practice the kids found us anyway. The house's beauty was itself a double-edged sword: the floors, the stairs, the furniture were all things our children seemed interested in destroying. I found myself yelling at them to not eat on this or jump on that. I had to tape off the stairs to the ground floor so that Ilya wouldn't break his neck on them. As for the backyard, it was very nice to have a backyard. But you still had to get the kids dressed in order to go out in it: in late March and early April, it was pretty cold out in New York. And you still had to be out there with them, trying to keep them entertained. Raffi was now four and a half, Ilya one and a half. They were still too small to just leave to their own devices.

The weekend we moved, Ms. V. started sending us small homework assignments, along with the daily schedule of what they did at school, so that we could start approximating it at home. She made it sound so easy. At 8:20, the kids arrived. Until 8:50, they got settled and wrote their names on a piece of lined paper. Then there was the "morning meeting," at which they listened to the song of the week and talked about their feelings. Then they had their first free time, during which they could play with blocks or pretend to be doctors. Then they went outside for half an hour. Then they had a snack and learned about nature or the seasons or the days of the week. And soon the day was over.

Ms. V. did this with eighteen kids, every single day. How hard could it be for us to do it with one kid, our own?

It turned out to be impossible. Raffi would sit still for a minute, trying to write his name on the lined piece of paper, but then he'd grow bored and want to find something in the refrigerator to eat, or to chase after Ilya, or to just run away and hide. Eric and Rachael's beautiful kitchen was bisected by a giant wood-topped island. It was convenient for eating and talking and doing homework; we could clean up from breakfast or read the latest COVID updates on our phones while urging Raffi to write his name or draw a picture about the seasons. Raffi liked sitting at the kitchen island well enough, but unfortunately, because it was pretty high off the ground, he had to sit on a barstool, and because he couldn't keep himself from fidgeting, he would periodically fall off his stool. From upstairs, it sounded like all hell was breaking loose. If you were in the room when it happened, it was just surprising. "Can you stop doing that?" I kept asking, as Raffi got up from another tumble, wounded and embarrassed and saying, "Ouch, ouch, ouch." But he could not stop doing it.

We wanted Raffi to do his schoolwork, but he was four years old. Yelling at him to sit still and write his name didn't work; bribing him with snacks worked, but only temporarily. By this point we had split the day in two, with one of us taking the morning shift with the kids and the other taking the afternoon. Emily, when she had the morning shift, had a few terrible days of homeschooling and gave up; I had a few terrible days and soldiered on. But we both agreed that the best thing to do was get both boys outside and keep them there as long as possible. Luckily we were just a few blocks from a small city park. We'd go there in the morning. In the afternoon, after lunch or nap, we'd go into the backyard. But the days seemed incredibly long. We felt very isolated. And we were scared.

In the evenings, after the kids were finally in bed, I searched for signs of societal collapse. Our new neighborhood was eerily silent. If someone broke into our house, it wasn't clear that any of our neighbors would know or care. And it was hard to tell, sitting in our house, what was happening beyond what I could see out my window. The father of M., the boy Raffi always played with on the playground after school, posted a photo on Facebook of his car with its windows smashed. The next day he sent me a photo of another car, on the same street as Ilya's preschool, also smashed. Some of my friends warned direly of supply-chain breakdowns. And I kept an eye on the news for states sealing their borders. That's what always happened in the disaster movies. Rhode Island, I read, was beginning to stop all people with New York license plates and forcing them to sign an agreement that they would quarantine for fourteen days. Florida was intercepting New Yorkers at its airports. We could still leave New York, but it felt like the window of opportunity was closing; I started wondering again whether we should get in the car and go.

During those first weeks of the lockdown, our days were filled with the park, attempted schoolwork, and Raffi falling off his stool. The rest of the time was filled with dread. Ms. V.'s song of the week those first couple of weeks was "Three Little Birds" by Bob Marley. One of the few things I successfully managed from the school curriculum was to play it over and over for Raffi on the Bluetooth speaker. I liked playing the song for him because, while he wasn't saying anything to this effect, I did suspect that he was scared. Sometimes I would sing it to him, after picking him up from one of his barstool tumbles. "Don't you worry," I would sing, "about a thing. / 'Cause every little thing / is gonna be all right." "Stop it, Dada," he would say, because he did not like my singing. I would stop. No reason to force your singing on someone. And anyway, I wasn't so sure that every little thing was going to be all right. Every night in the silent house, we heard sirens. Several times those first weeks, the sirens were on our street. Some of our neighbors, whom we did not yet know, were disappearing into the maw of the medical system. The father of one of my close friends from college was in the hospital on a ventilator.

IN RETROSPECT, MAYBE WE shouldn't have relocated. Maybe we shouldn't have tried to keep doing our schoolwork. Maybe we should have gone to the Cape. It was hard to tell how things would play out. I somehow kept thinking they would open the schools again at any minute.

The class Zooms now began for Raffi—every morning we would sit him down in front of the computer and try to get him to pay attention to his classmates and Ms. V. The Zooms were tantalizing, in their way, a glimpse of what socializing could mean, the faces of all the children on the screen, their parents hovering in the background, and our beloved Ms. V. trying to keep everyone interested and entertained. The Zooms were also nerve-racking, because we never knew how Raffi would react, whether he would sit still, whether he would speak when called on. The first few Zooms were spent arguing with him over the background (our computers were too old to support them). He was too little to sit in front of a computer like this! But the other kids were doing it somehow, or so it seemed. One time Raffi was behaving so badly that I shut the computer. I thought this was a punishment—tough but fair—but all it taught him was that you could make the whole thing go away. He started shutting the computer whenever he grew bored.

It was kind of fun to see people's houses over Zoom. You could often tell just from looking over the parents' shoulders whether they lived in a brownstone or an apartment. (We, of course, who lived in an apartment, were pretending for the moment to live in a brownstone.) A few people in the class had already decamped to their upstate homes. But it was also very sad. We had finally entered the part of the school year when the kids knew one another well enough to have playdates. Now it was unclear when we'd see those kids again.

We kept going to the park every morning, but during those first weeks it was also a place of fear. On one trip we saw a dead bird; a day later, a dead squirrel. In ordinary circumstances, this would be kind of grody and cool; at the time it felt like an omen. The first week we were in the Crown Heights house, the basketball hoops were still up on the courts and the playground inside the park was still open. Kids were playing in it. We had been told that COVID lived on surfaces, such as playground equipment, so I repeatedly had to pull Ilya, in particular, away from the entrance; he had no idea why he wasn't allowed to go inside. Then one day the city took down the basketball hoops; a few days later, they finally closed the playground. At the time, I was glad that they did this. But our world was shrinking.

The pressure the lockdown put on our marriage was intense.

You're not supposed to be everything to your partner, but under conditions of lockdown there was no choice. Our fights bloomed, extended themselves further into time, took on new forms.

The only fight we'd previously had about school was over how hard we should try to be on time in the morning. That fight was over—there was no school for us to try to be on time for. Now we had much more elaborate fights over how hard to press Raffi to actually do the homework Ms. V. assigned, the bare minimum of which was writing out the alphabet and the numbers up to twenty. The idea was to prepare the kids for kindergarten, where writing a backward seven would be frowned upon. Emily wasn't buying it. "I don't care if he writes a seven backward!" she kept saying. "He's four years old!" I did not disagree with that, exactly. But I thought we should at least try to stay tethered to our school, to Ms. V., to Raffi's classmates, and writing the numbers and letters seemed to me one of the ways we could do so. And, less social-emotionally, I didn't want him falling behind and showing up to kindergarten with his backward sevens when everyone else was already comfortably writing to twenty.

We both feared him losing interest in school. Emily feared he would lose interest if we pressed him too hard. I feared he would lose interest if he fell behind and grew discouraged. Neither of us had any way of knowing which of us was right. We were cut off from an actual school; it was just us and Raffi and Ilya in that house.

Andrew Cuomo, the not-yet-disgraced governor of New

York, had begun his press conferences, and a few times during my work shift I listened in. Here was a reasonable person, it seemed. Not a particularly appealing one, full of bluster and bad politics, but overall, compared to the president, reasonable. The day after it was reported that Rhode Island was pulling over people with New York license plates, Cuomo said that this was illegal. "They can't do that," he said. "I will sue Rhode Island." I liked that. It was aggressive but also legalistic, a remnant of the old world, when the way to get things done was to sue for them. Rhode Island responded, equally legalistically, by saying that it was pulling over *all* cars with out-of-state license plates. Fine. The episode demonstrated that there were rules and people were playing by them. And our house did not get broken into. Our new neighbors started recognizing us on the street and saying hi. We bought some flowers at the farmers market and planted them in the backyard.

During these weeks, Ms. V. assigned the kids a "report" for Women's History Month. You could choose a family member, she said, your mother or grandmother, or a notable woman from history, and then in front of the class, over Zoom, you had to tell everyone about her. Two days before it was due, Raffi and I sat down and read some brief educational books about Harriet Tubman, Clara Barton, Amelia Earhart, and Rosa Parks. Raffi waffled a bit, and I asked him whether he wanted to interview his mother or grandmother. When he said no, I pushed for Amelia Earhart . . . she had the right spirit of adventure and danger for Raffi, I thought. We read another book that we found online, then watched some short videos. When I tried to get him to watch a grown-up documentary, he balked.

At the park the next day, Raffi picked out a big stick and brought it home and made a "sculpture" of Amelia Earhart. It did not in any way resemble a person, much less Amelia Earhart, but I was impressed that he had thought of making a sculpture from a big stick. That day we also listened to some songs about Amelia Earhart. Raffi was fascinated by the fact that she had disappeared over the Atlantic Ocean. He kept asking us if she'd died. "Probably," we said. "She drowneded?" he asked. Probably, we said. He found this to be very interesting information.

Just six months earlier, Raffi had become obsessed with death. He asked us about it all the time and even talked Emily's mom into taking him to a local cemetery when we were visiting his grandparents in Maryland. (It happened to be the cemetery on Rockville Pike where Zelda and F. Scott Fitzgerald are buried.) Now death was everywhere—in our conversations, on the radio, in the ambulances streaming to the hospital—but it did not quite register for him. He did not see a connection between death as a concept in which he was interested and death that had now come for the old and vulnerable. That was a good thing. We knew of kids his age who were afraid to go outside, or afraid of contact with others, or somehow otherwise afraid, but that never happened to him. Raffi was not nearly as scared of the King Germ as we were, and never would be.

The time finally arrived for our big class Zoom on Women's History Month. It came during my shift, and I felt great trepidation as it approached. Would Raffi be able to sit through the whole thing? If so, would he be able to keep himself from saying something inappropriate about Amelia Earhart and her untimely death? And how would he react if, as was very likely, someone else had also chosen Amelia Earhart? Would he get mad and slam the computer shut? And then there was me to worry about: How would *I* react when everyone else's project was superior to ours, demonstrating their greater commitment to their children and their ability to keep their shit together even when the world was falling apart? I wouldn't put it past these parents to have guided their children to Pulitzer Prizes. I was very worried on all these fronts.

All eighteen kids showed up to the Zoom. The first boy to go was R., one of the charismatic leaders of the class, also the same R. that Raffi had punched in the stomach in late January.

For the women's history project, R. said, he had drawn a squirrel. He showed us the drawing. But it wasn't an ordinary squirrel, he said. It was a demon squirrel! And here were its scary demon ears and its scary demon eyes. He kept going on and on about the demon squirrel, and it took a while for everyone, including Ms. V., to realize that this had nothing to do with Women's History Month.

Finally, she stopped him. "You did an interview with your mom," she said. She knew this because R.'s very organized parents had sent her a video of this interview. "Do you remember anything from that?"

R. thought earnestly for a second and then said no.

And on it went. The kids were four and five years old; no one blew us away with their erudition and command of the subject matter. Two kids had chosen Michelle Obama, and two had chosen Rosa Parks, but no one else had chosen Amelia Earhart. Toward the end of the meeting, it was Raffi's turn. Right away he froze up, but Ms. V. coaxed it out of him. "What job did Amelia Earhart have?" she asked. "Was she a veterinarian?" "She was a pilot!" Raffi said. And he managed to say that she had crossed the Atlantic Ocean. So far, so good. Ms. V. decided to push him just a little bit more. "What is one more thing you can tell us about her?" she said. Raffi thought about it. I was sure he was going to launch into a dark monologue about how Amelia Earhart had "drowneded" in the ocean, but instead, the thing that popped into his head was that, when she was little, she had built a kind of ramp in her backyard and ridden off it in a wooden box, showing her early daredevil nature. It had been mentioned in both books we read, as well as in a PBS Kids cartoon we'd watched. "OK," said Ms. V. "Is that something that you want to build in *your* backyard?" It was a more complicated question than she realized, though she soon learned. "I could build it *here*," said Raffi, meaning at Eric and Rachael's house, "but at our real house where we live there's no room. But we're going to ask the construction workers to move into the house across the street, when they're done. Because when they're done we won't be able to see J.'s house. J. was my friend from preschool. J. and A. were my friends. So we always need to see J.'s house." Then he stopped. It was an amazing performance, a meditation on friendship and real estate and New York City, and by far the longest thing Raffi had ever said in a class Zoom. I was very proud of him. "Wow," said Ms. V., "thank you for that, Raphael. Kiss your brain!" But I was already kissing him on the forehead. We had survived the class-wide Zoom! And I felt like I had lost about two years off my life.

That day, we got word from Eric and Rachael that they were coming back to Brooklyn. We were momentarily devastated, though as soon as we got back to our apartment and our neighborhood, we found to our surprise that we were happier. It was our crappy stuff, our view of a giant construction site out the window, our weird neighbors. We no longer had to worry about what the kids were doing to Eric and Rachael's couch, and their refrigerator, and the floor. "We can eat on this couch, right?" said Raffi. Yes. That couch wasn't ever going to look good again. They could eat on it all they wanted.

I went back to Eric and Rachael's one last time with Raffi to clean up. It took all day. Raffi helped out for a while and then grew bored. I had no choice but to let him watch five straight hours of television. While cleaning I got word from my friend from college that his father had died of COVID. He was seventy-five years old and had five little grandchildren.

BY THE TIME WE GOT HOME, on April 10, the very worst of the pandemic was ending in New York City. People were still dying, but the hospitalizations had plateaued. Some people were beginning to leave their homes again and walk around. I no longer thought that society was going to collapse. I no longer even thought we'd get sick. Now the long slog of the lockdown began.

In the grand sweep of historical time, it wasn't very long at all—just three months: April, May, and June. But it took forever. We still did the day in shifts and we still tried to keep up the pretense of Raffi's schoolwork, mostly because we didn't want to disappoint Ms. V. And we continued to go to the park each day—our apartment was close to Fort Greene Park, so every morning we took the kids there. The playgrounds were closed but there was a big dirt field for the boys to play in, and a rock to climb on, and trees to stand under when it rained. The weather still wasn't great in the middle of April, cold and drizzly, but we stayed out as long as we could. Fort Greene Park is right next to Brooklyn Hospital, which was now using mobile morgues to keep up with the dead bodies. But the kids didn't know that, and I tried not to think about it too much.

It was hard: the constant presence of the children, the worry about the virus, and, above all, the isolation. Emily compared it to the first few months postpartum. But at least back then we had known approximately when it would end. Here, we had no idea. Though our shift schedule theoretically meant that we each had some time to work, neither of us ever got much work done. *Perfect Tunes* came out April 14—a terrible moment, as it turned out, for a new book. With no book tour, Emily gamely did a number of Zoom events nominally at bookstores across the country. The boys and I joined a few of the Zooms, though

Raffi kept wanting to talk to Emily and couldn't understand why that was impossible. "Take me off mute, Dada!" he kept saying. "Take me off mute!"

We kept arguing about Raffi's schoolwork. Emily thought we should drop out of Zoom school and develop our own park-based curriculum; I thought I was too lazy to develop my own curriculum, and anyway, Ms. V. had already developed one. Emily accused me of trying to get an A in pre-K. It was true I wanted an A.

It's incredible to think, in retrospect, of how many people were going through all these same things at the exact same time. But no two situations were exactly alike. From a childcare perspective, having two little kids who needed our nonstop attention was hard. But at least our kids weren't older and depressed. Ilya, for example, was too young to have friends and he *loved* spending time with us and with Raffi, and even Raffi didn't really mind the situation, though the lack of structure was hard on him. In truth, though, I don't know—it's going to take a lot of time to sort through all the damage.

I thought a lot about school during this period. The experience of actually being in the school, both pre-pandemic and now, was so different from my abstract and political conception of the schools when I was visiting them a year earlier. Yes, schools were a site of political contention and could be a site of political praxis. They made up a third of the New York City budget, by far the largest line item. It *did* matter where you sent your kid to school. But once you were inside, all you wanted was for the teacher to be nice to your kid, for the other kids to be nice to your kid. Of course you also wanted the school to be open.

One thing I hadn't understood about our school, when all I saw in it was a racial utopia, was how strict and traditional it was. That the kids wore uniforms, however disguised (their blue bottoms could be jeans; their white tops could have designs on them), was one sign. That the school's test scores were phenomenal was another. Some older parents I knew dropped occasional hints, but I wasn't listening. Now that we were in a global pandemic, the rubber started to meet the road. Ms. V. was a charismatic but extremely demanding teacher: she wanted our kids to do their homework, make it to the Zooms, and get ready for kindergarten. I understood where she was coming from, but we were at that moment somewhere else.

In the midst of these questions about school, I set up a phone call with my favorite teacher from my childhood, Ms. Lynch. I had had her in second grade in Driscoll School in Brookline, Massachusetts. I remembered her class many years later because we never sat at desks, but on the rug; she had us keep journals, in large black notebooks, which I filled with stories of alien invasions and supernatural feats. I had never had a classroom experience like that and would not again until I was in high school. It was one of the reasons that I became a writer. In fact, I had Ms. Lynch's contact information because, when my first book came out, she had sent me a generous and encouraging note.

Over the phone, Marcia Lynch told me her story. She had grown up in rural Massachusetts and then attended a highly progressive teachers college in Boston in the 1970s; she recalled a professor taking the class out into an abandoned lot not far from the school and asking the students to think of how they would teach a history class in that spot. She told me about how, fresh off this experience, she had started at a fairly traditional elementary school in one of the working-class towns of the South Shore. She brought with her the methods she'd developed in grad school: journaling, no desks, a democratic classroom. "My principal thought I was crazy," she said, "though he put his own kids in my class, so I guess I wasn't that crazy." After a few years there, she left for a job in the prestigious and progressive Brookline system, and in September 1982, Lynch started at Driscoll. My second-grade class was the first one she had. We sat on the rug and wrote in our journals. Ms. Lynch told me she could learn a lot about the kids from those journals—from how much violence there was in their stories about aliens and monsters, from who did (and did not) come to the rescue in them. As we wrote, Ms. Lynch would walk around the classroom, occasionally looking at what we were doing, often patting and sometimes kissing us on the head.

I think I was looking for permission from Ms. Lynch to stop attending the Zooms. She gave it to me. She said the pandemic presented a unique challenge to children. It was hard for them to understand why everything had changed so quickly, and why they weren't supposed to touch people, and why they couldn't see their friends and grandparents. She very much took Emily's side on the question of backward sevens. She said that kids' minds develop so fast that there is no use in hurrying them— what is difficult at age four will become easy at age five, and what is difficult at five will be easier at six. The skill to nurture instead was curiosity.

I was sitting in our car, parked on Bergen Street, as we had this conversation. A light rain was falling. Ms. Lynch went on to talk about how the moment I was in school, the early 1980s, was in some ways a golden age for progressive experimentation in the public schools; how not long after, the testing regime started to come into effect, first on the state level, then on the national one. Testing became a gateway to more funding for some schools, and a death sentence for others. Lynch hated it. For her it was a waste of teachers' time, of their creativity, and a waste of children's time as well.

But she also said that given a choice between an all-white progressive school where kids sat on the rug and an integrated school where they wore uniforms, we should go with the integrated school. We thought so too.

I got home after my phone call to find Emily and Raffi in a lousy mood. They'd had a big tussle over the numbers and letters. Raffi had agreed to write his name, Emily told me, and then for the letters he wrote out *A* and drew an apple, but further than that he would not go. By the time I took over, Raffi was due his reward in the form of some afternoon TV. "Dada," Raffi said to me, "since you are more serious than

Mama, I will watch *Wild Kratts*. Mama says that makes my brain less squishy."

We had convinced him that watching too much TV makes your brain squishy. But if you had to watch TV, *Wild Kratts* was a good thing to watch. I helped Raffi turn it on and then pulled out my laptop to write a report to Ms. V. on what educational things we'd managed to do that day. In the next few weeks, we did not give up on Raffi's schoolwork entirely, but we did pull back a little. We also cut back on the Zooms. When we told Ms. V. that we wanted to spend more time in the park and less time on the computer, she gave us her blessing.

THOUGH MANY PEOPLE HAD left town, and some were quarantining so hard that they did not venture out of their homes, we still saw at the park a great variety of parents. It was more intense, more revealing, than what one had seen, once upon a time, at the playground. The parents were trapped with their kids, and the kids were trapped with their parents. Everyone who had a nanny had sent their nannies home.

I saw a father, a big guy about my age, constantly losing his temper with his two-year-old daughter, who seemed not to want to play soccer with him. "Come on!" he pleaded. "This is our time to play together!" I saw a mother lose her temper with her eight- or nine-year-old, who was making some kind of unreasonable request that I did not hear. "Don't you start with me!" said the mother, holding up her hand in front of her daughter's face as if to ward off her demands. "I have spent *all day* doing things for you, all day, and . . ." and they kept walking through the park, out of earshot. As for me, I also yelled at the boys in the park, especially at Raffi. But at least I did it in Russian.

Gradually people started to relax. For some, this meant bringing back their nannies—you'd be talking to a parent in the park and the next day their kid would still be there but the parent would have been replaced by a middle-aged Latin American woman. For others, including us, it meant letting their kids play with their friends again. Starting in early May we saw A. and his father pretty much every day, and soon we added a third boy their age, G., whose father, a science professor, we met in the park, and together the three of them climbed all over the place and smashed into one another, and one day G. picked up a large stick and, at Raffi's urging, swung it at Raffi's head. "I thought I could duck," Raffi said later, though at first he bawled and had blood pouring down his face and a pretty impressive gash on his forehead. And yet I felt, as I carried him up to the ranger's station to get some iodine on his cut and a Band-Aid, like he was getting his childhood back.

On May 25, a former college basketball player and drifter named George Floyd, who had lost his job as a nightclub security guard because of the pandemic, used a fake twenty-dollar bill to pay for a pack of cigarettes at a convenience store in Minneapolis. The store's manager called the police, who then proceeded to kneel on Floyd's neck as he lost his breath, pleaded for help, and died. A teenager named Darnella Frazier filmed the killing.

Four days later, during my work shift, I watched the video. It seemed to last forever. Floyd cried for help but the people there who wanted to help him were told, by the police, to stay back. He died calling for his mother.

That evening, there was a protest in front of Barclays Center. I decided to go, and since it was during the part of the day when Emily was cooking dinner and wanted the fewest possible people bothering her, I took Raffi. Our building was right behind Barclays, and the police had blocked off our street and turned it into a staging ground. As we walked to the protest with our handmade signs, one of the policemen made a comment to me, suggesting that Raffi was too little to go to a protest. I was in a foul mood already and I turned and yelled at the guy. For a moment, it felt good; then it felt bad. Raffi didn't say anything, but I think it freaked him out. For the rest of the protest he clung to me and soon we left. This was the first of the anti-police protests in New York, and the mood was angry. People were standing in front of the police line yelling "Fuck the police!" You could tell things were going to deteriorate. I bought Raffi an ice cream to eat after dinner and we went home.

The protests were many things for many people; for us, they were the end of the lockdown. We still had the kids all day, and we still took them to the park, but now all of a sudden there were people around. And not just people but protesters. Our soulless neighborhood was now an epicenter of resistance to the police state. Almost every night from our window we could see a protest making its way down Atlantic. One night, seeing another protest moving down the avenue, Raffi shouted "Black lives matter!" out the window. We were proud of him.

We had some tough conversations during this time about race and the police, some of which were productive, some of which were dead ends. Raffi's superhero shows always depicted the police as incompetent at best, corrupt and dangerous at worst, and he had certainly heard no praise of the police in our house, but there was still enough pro-police propaganda on TV (the show *PAW Patrol*, for example) that he was surprised when we told him that the police regularly harassed and even shot Black people and poor people. "Why are the police acting like bad guys?" Raffi said. "They're supposed to save the day!" When we explained that the police had a history of racist behavior, he asked why there were Black people on the police force. (That was a good question; we suggested that maybe they were trying to improve the police from within.) And then he suddenly realized that his best friend from pre-K was Black. "What if they shoot T.?" he asked. "They don't shoot kids," I said to that one. "Actually," said Emily, "sometimes they do." Finally, seeing that we weren't much help, Raffi asked me to show him a picture of George Floyd. That was something I could manage. I pulled up a picture of George Floyd on my phone. Then he asked me to show him a picture of another man I had told him about, Eric Garner. Together, on my phone, we looked quietly at a photo of Eric Garner.

THE SCHOOL YEAR ENDED on Zoom. The camp we'd hoped Raffi would attend opened. Ilya's preschool also reopened. For two months we had something resembling normal life, at least as far as the kids were concerned. Raffi at camp was very shy at first, and in photos the counselors sent us, he always wore his mask, even outside, where it was not mandatory, as if using it to hide behind. But eventually he adjusted, made friends, got up to no good with them. Toward the end of camp, I even got a call from the counselor to tell me about Raffi's misbehavior. I pretended to be mad at him, but secretly I was relieved.

I have wondered frequently since the worst of it whether I learned any "lessons about parenting" from those three long months of lockdown and isolation, or from the year after that, when, overall, we spent way more time with our kids than we would have ordinarily. And the answer is that I'm not sure.

Raffi proved overall to be far, far more resilient than we had expected. He moved to Eric and Rachael's house without complaining; he entered lockdown with us; he wore his mask. When we arranged some meetings outside with his grandparents, whom he loves so much and whose absence from his life for the first months of the pandemic was one of the most disruptive things about it, he expressed joy at seeing them and hugged them. Though we were running out of money, we did not regret spending a week upstate in a cabin in the woods with our friend Rebecca and her two daughters, C. and N., whom Raffi loves. He would speak about that vacation for months to come, referring to it as the time we didn't have to wear "maskes" (pronounced "mask-is").

Summer ended and then school, fitfully and awkwardly, maskes on, began. At first it was just two days a week, but after a while it was more. What had struck us during the lockdown as our school's rigidity, its hyper-seriousness, now came in handy. There was not a school we knew of that was more committed to staying open, to making sure as many kids as possible were in-person as much as possible. The school set up separate classes for children of essential workers and children in difficult circumstances, so they could be in school full-time, and they pushed the boundaries of the COVID rules to get the rest of the kids up to full time as soon as they could. By December, they had managed to do it. It was wonderful that school was open, and wonderful, too, what happened there. Raffi's kindergarten teacher, Ms. C., was delighted with Raffi. She loved his monologues about animals, how quietly he played with his new friend S., how shy and gentle he seemed to be. And we were delighted with her. We kept waiting for the other shoe to drop, for Raffi to start acting out as he had in pre-K, but it never happened. He hadn't turned into an angel, but he was keeping it under control. One day I asked him why he wasn't getting in trouble the way he had in Ms. V.'s class. He said simply, "I'm older now and I know better." Once the school year regularized, in the spring, things got even better. Raffi thrived on following a schedule, on knowing what was going to happen next. "Today was exactly what I expected it to be," he said happily one day when I picked him up from after-school.

It's hard to tell now where our parenting ends and the pandemic begins. Raffi was four and a half when the COVID lockdown began and is past six now. He has had two birthdays during the age of COVID: one over Zoom, which we survived, and another in the park, with most of the adults vaccinated and unmasked, but most of the kids still masked, out of habit, and that birthday was a lot of fun.

Ms. Lynch had said to me during our phone call that maybe someday I'd look back on this period and think: "I got to spend so much time with them." That is, with the boys. "Now I never get to spend time with them." I'm sure she was right, that I will someday feel that way. But right now it just feels like a scar across our lives.

The other day we took the kids on a ferry ride along the East River. We paid our fare, wore our masks, and passed by that Fairway we had gone to on the last day of school. Now apparently it is a Food Bazaar. From the parking lot, and from inside, it had always loomed so large. From the water, though, it seemed small. I watched it recede. I don't think we will ever go there again.

Game Time

I remember this: Raffi in the community garden. He is maybe two years old. I have brought along a soccer ball. He likes running back and forth in the garden, attacking people's vegetables. Why not kick the ball while he's at it? He is willing to do it. At first, he is always willing to do it. But he is not good at it. He misses the ball more often than he hits it. In order to keep him interested, I make a goal out of my legs. When, after numerous attempts, he finally scores, I pick him up and spin him around to celebrate. After that he doesn't want to kick the ball anymore; he just wants to get picked up and spun around.

We attend a party at a friend's house out in New Jersey. There are a lot of kids. Raffi is maybe a year old, part walking, part crawling. There is another boy there about his age, skinnier, less beautiful, and yet the way he crawls, the way he picks up toys, I can immediately see that he has total control of his body. That is what it looks like, then. Raffi will continue to occasionally trip over his feet until well past his fifth birthday.

But it is hockey that I most want him to learn, and that is a sport for which you don't have to be a graceful walker. Bobby Orr was bowlegged. I buy Raffi skates off Craigslist the summer he turns two and take him skating at a rink in Queens a little while later. He clings to me the entire time we're on the ice and cries when I try to put him down. We skate around a few times and then go home. The next time we try, he spends a little more time with skates on ice, but tears soon follow, and again we go home.

The first time he doesn't cry when skating is that winter at my father's house on the Cape. My father has a small pond next to his house, which freezes after a few nights of cold. We put our skates on inside and then walk down to the pond through the woods. Emily takes a video. Raffi is barely able to stand on his skates, but he is so surprised at this whole turn of events, us on a pond, in the woods, in the winter twilight, that he just takes it in. My dad's giant dog, now fully grown, comes out onto the ice with us. I hold Raffi under the armpits and slowly skate him around. He doesn't mind.

I say he doesn't mind because as I write this it's hard to get Raffi to do anything. He doesn't want to go outside, he doesn't want to learn how to Rollerblade, he definitely doesn't want to go ice skating. He wants to play with his Transformers and watch *Wild Kratts* on TV. Noble pursuits, to be sure, but there is more to life. Did I do something wrong, or was it always going to be this way? I can't tell.

EMILY AND I HAD a big fight once about sports. I can't remember what started it but that's not the point—our fights are ambient, the product of a certain level of humidity. The humidity rises for a while and then it rains.

In this fight it emerged that Emily did not see the point of sports. She thought they inculcated violence and were implicated in rape culture. She wanted Raffi to stay away from them. Nor did she think he had shown any aptitude for sports, and pressuring him to play was only going to backfire. "It's going to bite you in the ass," she said.

I disagreed. He was never going to enjoy sports if he was bad at them. He needed a baseline level of competence—knowing how to skate, how to kick a soccer ball, how to throw a baseball. After that he could decide what he wanted to do. As for rape culture, as for male violence, sports actually helped sublimate those things. The kids who came in and shot up their schools were not athletes. They were loners who played too many video games. The athletes got shot by those kids! And then I said something that I wish I had not said, but it was what I felt, which was: "Boys play sports! That's what boys do!"

Having gotten me to say something stupid, Emily declared victory and left the room.

What had I actually meant to say? Perhaps I had meant to say: I, a boy, had played sports my whole life, and they had meant so much to me. I played them when I was little—hockey, soccer, baseball, as long as it was a sport, as long as I was running around. I played them as a teenager, now more seriously—football and hockey. And then it was hockey that I picked up again, in grad school, when I was miserable and at loose ends after the end of my first marriage; and hockey that I played when I moved to New York after grad school; and hockey again when I was lonely and lost in Moscow, living with my grandmother.

When I was a kid, sports were something my father and I had in common. My father has never been a big talker. He is mostly silent, thoughtful, active. We never talked about girls or books (I talked to my mother about books), but he drove me to all my games, and on the way home sometimes he would make a comment. One time in youth hockey he suggested I shoot the puck more. And one time when I was preparing for a tennis tournament, and my coach seemed worried that I wouldn't be able to handle losing, my father said on the ride home, "He doesn't know that you've been both the best player on your teams and the worst." Meaning: "You know how to handle adversity." It was the highest compliment he ever paid to my character.

Most of the friends I have made in life I made through sports. Most of the most powerful memories in my life have been sports memories. My first encounter with what I now recognize to be philosophy was through sports, in the figure of my high school football coach, a retired biology teacher named Aredis Kojoyian. During practice, Coach Kojoyian would sing the praises of the forearm shiver, legally the most effective way in a football game to knock someone over. This was philosophy of a kind. But after games, when he was called upon to explain what had happened (usually, that we had lost), Coach Kojoyian could be profound. "In any endeavor you undertake in life," he would begin, and then he would explain the value of hard work, dedication, and solidarity. He would explain, too, how these virtues were not always rewarded in real time. "The better team does not always win," he said once, after we had played our hearts out for him in a loss to a more talented group of players. "The better man does not always win." But you must persevere, Coach Kojoyian said. You must get up to fight again.

For a while, under the influence of Kojoyian, I came to believe that sports, and football especially, had special character-building properties. Physical labor, teamwork, discipline—the martial virtues without the martial vices. Of course, my experience of actual sports teams indicated that this was nonsense. Some of my teammates were wonderful people; some were jerks. I have played sports with plenty of loudmouths and bullies. They didn't shoot up any schools, but a lot of them went into finance.

Still, for me, sports had done so much and been so much. They were a world away from the world of work and status; I enjoyed playing them when I was one of the best people on the field or the ice, and also when I was one of the worst. Of the things from my own life that I felt I could give to Raffi, the one I most wanted to give him was sports.

THE FIRST THING YOU need to learn when learning to skate is how to get up after you fall. The natural way to get up is to

place one hand on the ground and lean on it for support. On the
ice, that doesn't work—your hand will slip and you will just fall
again. Instead, you need to get onto your knees, lift one of them
up, plant your skate directly under it, and push off that knee
with both hands. Now you're standing up and will be for a little
longer, until you fall.

The next thing to learn is that you skate on your edges, shift-
ing from the inside to the outside edge depending on what you
need to do. You can begin to learn this by lifting up your skates
and putting them back down again while standing still. At the
rink in Queens, or on my father's pond, and even a couple of
times on the tiny koi pond in our community garden, which
froze nicely when it was cold out, Raffi and I stood across from
each other and raised our hands like lions and stomped back
and forth from foot to foot, roaring at each other. That was our
edge work. Once in a while he fell and, in textbook fashion, got
up again.

But beyond that it got too complicated. Beyond that you had
to start moving. Ideally you would angle your feet out a tiny bit
and push off the inside edge, first from one skate, then the other.
This is easier said than done. I would try to explain it, and Raffi
would grow frustrated. I'd try to show him by doing it, but he
didn't like that either. Inevitably he would end up in tears—
from anger at his slow progress, or because he'd fallen and hurt
himself, or maybe just because he was cold. Sometimes, especially at the rink in Queens, he would lie down on the ice and
start eating ice shavings. "That's disgusting," I would say, because

people are always spitting and blowing their noses onto the ice, but that would only make him want to do it more. At that point I would feel I had reached the end of my pedagogical potential when it came to Raffi and ice hockey.

How did others do it? How had my father done it? He had been an amateur boxer in Moscow, and he'd stayed in shape well into his fifties. One of my few memories from before our emigration is of my father doing squats in our Moscow apartment.

But he never coached me or pushed me to play sports. He must have signed me up for all the teams I played on, and he drove me to all the games and practices, but I don't remember any pressure, I don't remember him ever sending me out into the yard to improve my game. He liked sports and was interested in sports, but what he really loved was math. If I asked my father a question about math, he would take out a sharp pencil and a notepad and start explaining it to me.

In the world of hockey, by far the most famous father of all time is Walter Gretzky. His parents were ethnic Ukrainians who came to Canada early in the twentieth century and became small farmers outside Brantford, Ontario, about an hour's drive south of Toronto. As a youth Walter was a talented hockey player, but he was too small and skinny to make the leap to the pros. After high school he went to work for Bell Telephone, setting up phone lines. He married young. In 1961, when he was twenty-two, he and his wife, Phyllis, had their first child, Wayne.

The story of Wayne Gretzky's youthful exploits has been told many times. Walter put him on skates when he was two and a half. Wayne seemed to love it. On Saturday nights, the family would go over to Walter's parents' farm and watch *Hockey Night in Canada*. Between periods, little Wayne liked to grab a small stick and practice shooting on his grandmother. The winter Wayne turned four, Walter built a rink in the backyard so Wayne could practice more. At the age of six, Wayne tried out for the youngest local hockey team—for ten-year-olds. He made the team. In that first season, he scored one goal. Four years later, as a ten-year-old, he scored 378. By then he was already famous in Canada as a hockey prodigy.

When he was fourteen, Wayne had to leave small-town Brantford because some of the other parents were being nasty: they called him a puck hog and booed when he scored. He moved to Toronto to play for a more competitive team; he lived with the family of one of his teammates and visited his parents on weekends. In his autobiography he recalled this period with regret. "Looking back on it, those years in Toronto were no way for a kid to live. I was awfully lonely, living with someone else's family, coming home on weekends, trying to feel part of my own family by talking to them on the telephone." But it worked out: five years after that move, at the age of nineteen, Wayne won the Hart Memorial Trophy, given to the most valuable player in the National Hockey League.

By then his father, Walter, was almost as much a celebrity as Wayne. After all, you couldn't up and become Wayne Gretzky. But you *could* become Walter Gretzky—that is, a man who encourages the talent of your progeny, who tends to it, who does enough to push it along without destroying it. And the question became: Just how much did Walter push Wayne?

Here, the narratives diverge. Wayne, in his autobiography, says he was hockey mad from a young age, wouldn't stop skating, and that ultimately Walter had no choice but to build a rink in the backyard. But Walter, in *his* autobiography, admits that he bought their house in Brantford, not long after Wayne was born, specifically because it had a flat yard that he could someday build a rink on. Wayne says he would skate on the rink in the morning before school, then after school, then after dinner, until his parents would yell at him to come in. But he also says that when he was little his father would make him sit with a notepad while he watched hockey games on TV and draw the game with a pencil as it happened, the better to develop his game sense. There was a push and pull, clearly—a driven father, a preternaturally gifted child—and it's impossible at this distance to know which of them predominated.

The saddest hockey story I know is that of a former NHL player named Patrick O'Sullivan. O'Sullivan's father, John, had been a minor-league hockey player who desperately wanted his son to make the NHL. To make that happen, O'Sullivan got his son on the ice early and often. He forced him to practice his stickhandling in the basement. He made him run alongside the car in his pads. And he regularly beat him up and yelled at him. "From the moment I got my first pair of hockey skates at five years old," O'Sullivan would later write, "I got the living shit kicked out of me every single day. Every day after hockey, no matter how many goals I scored, he would hit me."

This went on for a decade, through various teams in different cities, including the U.S. National Team Development Program in Ann Arbor, Michigan. To the younger O'Sullivan, the mystery was always why so few people tried to intervene in what was so clearly an abusive relationship. Later on, after he'd stopped playing, O'Sullivan tried to talk to some of his former coaches. The answer, overall, was that hockey parents were so crazy, it was hard to tell which of the parents were just a little bit intense, and which of them were stepping over the line into physical and mental abuse. The other answer was that O'Sullivan was a great player. He led the U.S. under-eighteen team to a gold medal in Slovakia in 2002 and was the leading scorer on his Canadian juniors team for four straight years. No one got involved, because whatever his father was doing, it seemed to be working. Patrick O'Sullivan could play.

The abuse only ended when Patrick, at sixteen, physically fought back. He lost the fight but managed to get to a phone and call the police. Then he filed a restraining order and moved in with a teammate whose father was a police officer.

The abuse ended, but the trauma remained. When it came time for the NHL draft, O'Sullivan, a first-round talent, dropped late into the second round, in part, he believed, because teams worried about his "baggage." In the end, O'Sullivan had a decent career in the NHL, playing more than three hundred games and scoring fifty-eight goals, but he bounced around from team to team and never really found a playing home.

The beloved father Walter Gretzky did not create the monstrous father John O'Sullivan, but there is still a straight line from one to the other. Children are their own people, yes, but they are also so much at our mercy—at the mercy of our moods, our insecurities, even our dreams.

WHEN RAFFI TURNED THREE and a half, we signed him up for a skating class at the rink in Queens. It was a terrific class. The teacher was a blond, six-foot-tall former college player. She was patient and imposing and beautiful, and Raffi loved her. Every time she gave him a compliment, he beamed. She had the kids hold a ball and skate with it; she had them skate along squiggly lines that she drew with a marker; she had them chase a soccer ball around the ice.

I loved the class and I loved the rink. I loved the musty, sweaty smell; the cold air; the lousy coffee you could get from a machine in a Styrofoam cup for seventy-five cents. And I loved what people did there: they played hockey.

I loved, too, the feel of being there with Raffi. There were so many places we went where I had to tell him not to do things: not rip out flowers in the community garden, not poke at dog poop on the sidewalk, not crash into other kids in music class.

When we were in our apartment there was hardly anything he could do. At the rink, it was different. It was a giant space with rubber mats on the floor. Raffi could shout if he was excited, run back and forth along the perimeter of the rink if he was energetic, climb up and down on the bleachers. No one cared. Getting all the skating stuff scheduled was a pain, getting Raffi out the door was a misery, traffic to the rink could sometimes be annoying—but once we got there, I felt like a burden had been lifted from my shoulders. I could relax.

But there was a scheduling issue. Raffi was in day care five days a week, and on Saturday mornings he went to Russian school, and now on Sunday mornings we had hockey. In theory, two non–day care activities did not seem unreasonable. But in practice it was a little much. Raffi was just three years old. Emily suggested we drop one of his weekend commitments. After some soul searching, I decided it had to be hockey.

In retrospect—I don't know. Raffi claimed to find Russian school boring and he cried the first two times I dropped him off. But it was three whole hours! On a Saturday morning! It was pretty much the only time I had that year to write. And Raffi made some nice friends.

But his progress in hockey stagnated. We still went skating, just he and I, but not nearly as often. When something isn't on the Google calendar, it loses its priority. Then Raffi shot up in height and went through a phase when he would get tangled up with his feet even more than usual. You'd be walking next to him and he'd just suddenly fall to the ground. Emily would look at me like, I told you so. "He has a future in the arts," her look would say. "Stop trying to turn him into a mighty athlete."

I TALKED TO OTHER DADS. My college roommate George, who had eaten a bag of Milano cookies while his wife gave birth, urged patience. He said his son had no interest in watching or playing sports until the day he turned six. Now, at seven, he was willing to watch any sport that was on TV and was constantly dragging George out of the house to throw a ball back and forth. My hockey friend Mike said his son was resistant to skating until the day he took him up to the small outdoor rink in Montreal where he himself used to skate as a kid and put him in full pads: helmet, elbow pads, hockey pants, shin pads. Armored up, indestructible, and on a rink with no time limits or pressure, his son finally got the hang of it and has been skating ever since.

My high school friend Loren told a more dramatic tale. He wanted his son to play soccer. At the age of four, the earliest opportunity, he signed him up for a team. But it turned out his son did not want to play. He would refuse to go in when the coach said it was his turn, and if he was cajoled or pressured into going in anyway, he would refuse to play: he would simply sit down in his own goal and stay there until the coach finally pulled him out. Loren, incredibly, kept taking him to the games. After all, they had paid their fee. By the end of the season, his son was still refusing to play in the games. What is more, he had infected the entire team with his philosophy of noncompliance—*all* of them were now sitting in their own net and not playing.

Loren told me this not long after that terrible season had ended. I was awed by his perseverance. We would surely have pulled Raffi out after a couple of games, just out of sheer embarrassment. And yet a few years later, I saw Loren again. His son was now eight. He had taken a year off and then had two fun seasons, playing along with everyone else, and had now made the travel team. The team played or practiced three times a week and then one day or even two days on the weekends. Loren's new problem was that there wasn't time left over for his son to do anything else.

I looked up some studies on children's participation in sports. The optimistic ones tended to come from Europe. They stressed the benefits of hard work and fresh air. The more pessimistic studies tended to come from the Anglo-American world. They depicted a sports culture in which kids were pushed to start too early and become too competitive. One study from New Zealand analyzed parental comments at youth sporting events. Nearly half were positive or encouraging, but almost as many were negative or scolding. The researchers pointed out that they had come up with a larger share of negative comments than previous studies because they classified "instructional" comments— "Pass the ball"; "Mark your man"—as negative. They classified them as negative because, according to still other studies, kids who are told how to do something do not learn it as well as kids who have to figure it out on their own. The New Zealand researchers described seeing little kids stopping in the middle of their games to try to hear the instructions their parents were yelling from the sidelines, and then attempting to carry out those instructions. I found this image poignant. I was so used to thinking of Raffi as a rebel, a noncompliant. Probably these parents were used to thinking of their kids that way as well. And yet these kids wanted to learn. They wanted to get it right. They stopped in the middle of the thing they were doing to try to listen. And the parents were screwing it up.

The more I read, the worse it got. American youth sports were in crisis, it turned out. The pressures of a winner-take-all society had filtered down into the games that children played. For a long time, working-class parents had seen sports as a potential path to a college scholarship; now middle-class parents saw them as a way into the Ivy League. *The Atlantic* published an incredible article about Connecticut parents who sought out niche sports like fencing to increase their kids' college chances. The magazine then had to retract the article because, they said, the reporter had lied to their fact-checker, but overall no one questioned the thesis. Youth sports were too competitive. In order to keep participating, kids had to spend more and more time playing them. My friend Loren wasn't the only one faced with a dilemma: either he devoted his eight-year-old's entire life to soccer, or he had to basically abandon soccer. There wasn't a lot of middle ground.

All of this was an argument against starting in on this stuff in the first place. And then I would watch Raffi with his friends, or with his little brother, or even with me. He wanted to wrestle with us, he wanted to run around, he wanted to jump off things and climb on them. This was not, to me, the behavior of a person who was uninterested in sports. To me it felt like he wanted to learn how to play. And yet at the same time he did not want to "learn" anything. Of his gym class in pre-K he complained that it had too many rules. Among his after-school activities, he said he preferred sculpture to soccer, presumably because there were fewer instructions. I couldn't figure out how to break through it. Thinking that Raffi might enjoy skating without all the rigmarole of getting to the rink, I bought him some Rollerblades. He tried them once, immediately fell down, and did not want to try them again. For months they sat unused in our closet, taking up precious space.

THERE IS NO TRAGEDY like the tragedy of the bedroom, Tolstoy told Gorky when they were both living near Yalta at the turn of the last century.

For Tolstoy, the tragedy of the bedroom was the tragedy of marriage, including his own marriage to Sophia Behrs. It was his inability to remain faithful to her even as they had thirteen children. It was his renunciation of lust as sinful even as he continued to experience it and give in to it. It was his failure to be a reliable husband for this one person even as he was so much to so many others.

Gorky appears not to have been very impressed by this statement. He thought Tolstoy feared and hated women. But I was impressed by it. For years I thought it was the most profound thing Tolstoy had ever said, that anyone had ever said. All the materials of literature—Tolstoy lists "earthquakes, epidemics, the horrors of disease, and all the agonies of the soul"—paled in comparison to the problems that could afflict two people left alone with each other in the same house, in the same bed, forever. They could cease to love each other; or they could misunderstand each other; or they could keep hitting their knees on the edge of the bed, because it was poorly designed. And all of it out of view of the world, in silence, with no one to talk to about it.

I still think it's a profound statement, but to me there is now a greater tragedy. When Raffi was a tiny, vulnerable infant, and I used to see in our neighborhood a fat, healthy ten-month-old who looked like he could eat our baby if he wanted to, I would feel only jealousy, a desire to be where that parent was, at a less vulnerable place than the place we were at. And I feel something similar now when I see a parent walking down the street with their older child—say, a ten-year-old. I want to be where they are. But I also feel like I see more. I see two people who have passed through a terrible struggle. Especially when I see the child holding a soccer ball or a baseball bat, I see the struggle for independence (for both of them), the struggle for connection, the parent's wish to teach something, the child's wish both to learn it and to leave. I think now that there is no tragedy like the tragedy of parenthood. There is no other thing you do in life only so that the person you do it for can leave you. When they leave, that is success; when they do something because they want to do it and not because you want them to do it, then you have done your job. You succeed when you make yourself irrelevant, when you erase yourself. Parents who fail to do that have failed. I feel myself failing in exactly this way every day.

What if Raffi likes something else, was destined to do something else? But if I don't try to teach him, how will he ever learn? One spring day, as I watched five-year-old Raffi and his friend try to master riding a bike, the other boy's father told me a sad tale of how he'd tried to teach his older son to ride. He is himself an avid rider, loves getting around the city in this way, but with his older son he had been hands-off, patient, empathetic, and then one day, when this had yielded no results, he pushed too hard. He scared his boy off. As a result, his now teenage son does not know how to ride a bike.

Mostly, though, the father blamed his equipment. He had been cheap and bought all his older son's bikes on Craigslist. He wasn't going to make that mistake again with his younger son. He was paying top dollar. But as of now, as we watched our boys try to ride, neither of them could do it. They'd pick the bike up, push themselves a little, try to pedal, then fall down. It was OK! They were only five. But soon they'd be six. And then seven. And when exactly would the moment come?

WHEN THE COVID LOCKDOWN began, in March 2020, and Emily and I were taking the kids to the park every day, I started bringing a soccer ball. I just shoved it into the little storage space at the bottom of Ilya's stroller. Once we arrived, I would take it out. Raffi would mostly ignore it. But we were spending so much time in the park, and there was so little else to do, that eventually he would deign to kick it a couple of times. Slowly, very slowly, he got better at it.

The hard part is figuring out where to plant your foot. The natural impulse is to place your foot far away from the ball, so that your other foot might have, so to speak, a running start. This is why a lot of kids fall down when they first try to kick a ball—they've planted their nonkicking foot too far away, and then their kicking foot swings short of the ball and upward, and the momentum carries them onto their back. Instead, you need to plant the foot right next to the ball; your kicking foot's maximum velocity is at the bottom of its downswing as it moves past the planted foot and into the leather. I only needed to tell Raffi this once. He didn't believe me at first, but then I saw him looking down and making an effort to plant his left foot correctly. The other thing I told him was not to kick with his toe. A soccer ball should be kicked with either the instep of your foot (i.e., your shoelaces), for power, or the inside of your foot, for accurate short passes. It took him a while to stop kicking with his toe, but I could see him consciously trying to do it the right way. It didn't happen overnight, but eventually, because there was so much time and so little else to do, Raffi got the hang of it. When a soccer ball is sitting still on a flat surface, Raffi can now give it a good whack. And in fact, when he sees a soccer ball, this is what he wants to do to it.

As for hockey, all the rinks closed in mid-March and stayed closed until the wintertime. But then some of them opened again. In fact, given the COVID restrictions in force in the city, everyone had to be outside all the time, and one of the few out-door activities was ice skating. For the first time in two years, I signed Raffi up for a hockey class; on weekends we frequently went skating. One time, even Emily came skating. The high-light was a birthday party for one of Raffi's classmates, held at the skating rink in Prospect Park. Raffi was the only one in his class who knew how to skate, and he loved going from class-mate to classmate and giving them instructions.

But we'd also had an experience over the summer that made a deep impression on me and my sports fantasies. Every day after Raffi's camp we would go get an ice cream near his bus stop and then hang out at a playground on the south side of Prospect Park. After that I would put him on my bike and we'd ride home. Unlike at the playgrounds near our home, Raffi didn't usually know anyone there, but it was large and shady and he liked it.

On the day I'm thinking of, soon after we arrived Raffi started talking to a kind of artsy-looking kid his age. He had long brown hair and big brown eyes and, though it was warm out, he was wearing jeans. I was standing nearby, and I heard the boy tell Raffi that all his friends had left the playground and the kids who remained weren't being nice to him. There were three beefy blond kids nearby, and they were roughhousing with one another. Raffi told the boy that he would stand up to the bullies, and true to his word he went over to the other boys and puffed himself up and roared at them. But the boys were unimpressed and chased Raffi away. He kept going over there, however, and eventually they just included him in their pushing and running game. The other boy sulked off, by himself, rejected again.

And almost despite myself, despite all my dreams of Raffi's sports future, I thought: Don't do it! Stay with the sad, artsy boy. He is your true friend! You will have far more in common with him. Don't waste your time with those other boys!

But there was nothing I could do about it—Raffi was not in the business of asking me whom he should play with—and I went and sat down on a bench at the other end of the playground. I thought back to my own childhood. I had always played sports, had always been the roughhousing kid on the playground, but at a certain point, around the start of high school, playing sports came to occupy more and more of my time. It determined what else I could do and whom I hung out with. And it created a thin layer of distrust between myself and some of the kids who shared my interests in literature and writing. I always felt like those were my people, and I had been separated from them.

When I got to college, I kept playing sports, especially football. This was, in retrospect, a mistake. I did it partly because I wanted to play more football, but also partly because of the stupid personal "code" I had developed in which football held pride of place as a testing ground for honor and courage. I spent two years on this, two valuable years, my first two years of college, two years of early morning football practice and weight lifting and film study and crashing my helmet into guys who weighed fifty pounds more than I did. In the spring of freshman year, I read *Waiting for Godot* for Professor Leo Damrosch's introductory English class with my head swimming from a concussion. During my sophomore year, it took me months of agonizing indecision before I finally quit. It was a conversation with my father that finally made up my mind. I was home for winter break and explaining to him my theories about football, how it was a place to demonstrate physical courage, how this was important in the life of a man, and he said something very interesting in response. "You know," he said, "after the war, a lot of the men who came back, who had been very physically brave in the fight against the Germans, proved to be total moral cowards in the face of political pressure" from Stalinism. My father, who had punched out anti-Semites on the streets of Moscow, thought that moral courage, which could not be cultivated on a football field, was much more important than physical courage, which maybe could. A few weeks later, I finally went into the coach's office and quit. The semester after I did that was the best semester of my life. I suddenly had so much time. That summer, I moved to Moscow, fell in love, stayed awhile, and started writing fiction in earnest for the first time.

In a certain reading of my life, sports have been a huge waste of time, a missed opportunity, an abrogation of my responsibility to myself and others.

Back at the playground, about five minutes after I sat down, Raffi came to me in tears. One of the blond boys had pushed him down really hard, and Raffi's breath had been knocked from him and his back scratched up. It took an uncommon amount of time for him to stop crying, and he even curled up in my lap for a few minutes, something he almost never did anymore, and certainly not in public. "I'm not going to play with those kids again," he told me toward the end of his crying jag. I agreed. We went over to the swings and I pushed him for a while, as high as he could go. His mood improved.

And then suddenly he said, "I want to leave. I want to leave right now!" I didn't know what had gotten into him, but I, too, was ready to leave, so I took him off the swing and then followed him to the exit.

His artsy friend, the one he had rejected, was also leaving; Raffi wanted to walk out with him; that's why he was in a hurry to go. When we caught up with him and his dad, Raffi told them all about how we always biked home from the playground together, and how his mom didn't ever get mad at him, and on and on. Then he very cutely said bye to the kid, and we went home. He had made a friend, the right friend, and he had done it much faster than I would have done. I was proud of him. On the ride home he regaled me with trivia about the Transformers Universe and asked me to rank the comparative size and strength of various animals. We had a good time.

Bear Dad

I had just turned six when we left the Soviet Union, and I remember very little about my parents, in particular my father, in that pre-emigration period. I remember him pulling me through the snow, on a sled, on the way to day care; I remember him and Masha going into a river, on a summer trip outside Moscow, and coming out with crayfish that we would roast on a fire. I remember him sitting at the kitchen table in our small apartment, drinking tea and reading. Once or twice, when I had really screwed up, he gave me a very reluctant and mostly ceremonious spanking. I thought of him as strict and demanding and loving and mostly silent. The one incident that has remained in my mind, probably because it is so shameful, is when my friend Grisha and I got into a fight with some boys in the courtyard in front of our building. The boys knocked Grisha down and started kicking him. Instead of helping, I ran to get my father. From the courtyard I called to him through the open window. He stuck his head out, I explained the situation, and he said, "Figure it out yourself." Then he shut the window. When I returned to Grisha, the other boys were already gone, he was picking himself up, and he was very angry that I hadn't done more to help.

"Figure it out yourself": in certain ways that was my father's lesson to me, though in other ways he was far more involved in my life than the fathers of other kids I knew. One time when I was around twelve and wanted to go skating with some friends on a freshly frozen local pond, my dad went out, measured the ice, and declared it unsafe. My friends made fun of me for a while after that, but I didn't mind: my father was stricter than their fathers, and I knew why. It was because he was Russian, and because he was an immigrant. Their fathers had golf, jokes, in some cases girlfriends (my friends' parents had a high rate of divorce). My father just had his family.

I spent the longest portion of my childhood in a suburb outside Boston called Newton. It was a nice town, full of professional families, many of them Jewish: Jewton, some of us called it. And we also were Jewish: that was the reason we'd been let out of the Soviet Union; that was the reason we'd left. But we were not like the Jews among whom we now found ourselves. These American Jews were rich where we were, or had been, poor, comfortable where we were maladjusted. Most of all they seemed soft—their clothes, their carpets, their faces. Whether they were actually as soft and comfortable as they seemed I now wonder, but at the time, I saw it clearly. The men in particular. They were not like our men, our fathers. Our fathers were tough. My dad had been an amateur boxer; his friend Yury Rapoport did karate and drove his car very fast. Misha Alperovich also did karate. The least butch and least macho of the Russian fathers I knew was tough in a different way. He was a former Soviet dissident. He had been attacked and threatened and run out of the Soviet Union by the KGB.

None of these fathers were violent men, nor were they large men. They were all about five foot six, mostly worked as computer programmers, and liked to play chess. But they had come from a violent place, and they had had to adapt to it. They *were* Russian in that sense, more Russian than Jewish. Though not, of course, in Russia.

We, their children, did well in school, mostly stayed out of trouble, and kept our eyes on the prize of college admission. This part I always attributed to our being Soviet, to the Soviet tradition of taking school seriously, of dressing up in uniforms and writing in tiny graph-paper notebooks. There was also my parents' own bookishness, especially my mother's: she had read everything ever written, as far as I could tell.

And I still think that played a part, though now I think it was a small part. Later on, as an adult, I met Soviet émigré children whose parents were a lot less bookish than mine, as well as immigrants from countries that were not the Soviet Union— and yet they were in most ways a lot like me. It was neither Soviet habits nor Jewishness that distinguished us and pushed us along. It was the emigration itself. I think what our parents managed to communicate to us, mostly without ever needing to put it in so many words, was the precarity of our existence. Most of us remember our mothers and fathers on the way to

America: the uncertainty of that process, the scariness of it. In the Soviet case, we stopped over in Austria and then Italy; our parents sold various things they'd brought so we could have some cash on hand. We remember what it was like when we first arrived in the United States and lived with friends or relatives, then in small apartments in tough neighborhoods. We remember our parents without jobs, looking for work, most of them eventually finding work but never feeling entirely comfortable there. We had scrambled our way into the middle class, but we knew in our bones that we could fall right out of it again. This was what our parents had taught us—not deliberately, not on purpose, but just by virtue of the journey they had taken us on.

I always think that Raffi can be like me. I want him to be better, and freer, and happier—but as a kind of baseline, *at least* like me. After all, he looks like me; he shares my name. But there is no way I can re-create for Raffi the experience of our emigration. Nor do I want to! I want him to have a stable, happy childhood, and I want him to stay friends forever with the kids he is friends with now. I want things to be easy for him. But I am beginning to see that this is not an unalloyed good; that it could have, in the end, its own costs.

Amy Chua's *Battle Hymn of the Tiger Mother* was a huge hit when it came out in the U.S. in 2011. People were offended, angry, but also fascinated: Is this how Chinese parents raise their children? Is this how to get your kid to Carnegie Hall (as the book's introduction says)—and from there to Harvard? Chua became a celebrity—both a victim and a beneficiary of American anxieties over the rise of China.

I was surprised when I finally read the book not long ago—it was much funnier and more self-aware than I'd expected. It was also scarier.

Battle Hymn offers itself as a kind of lesson in Chinese parenting. Here is how Western parents do it, Chua, a professor at Yale Law School, says over and over again, and here is how Chinese parents do it. Western parents are soft; Chinese parents are hard. Western parents are permissive and undemanding; Chinese parents are the opposite. "Even when Western parents think they're being strict," Chua writes, "they usually don't come close to being Chinese mothers. For example, my Western friends who consider themselves strict make their children practice their instruments thirty minutes every day. An hour at most. For a Chinese mother, the first hour is the easy part. It's hours two and three that get tough." Chua started her two daughters, Sophia and Lulu, on piano and violin lessons early and kept them at it. She describes her search in New Haven and then New York for the right teachers, her insistence that her daughters never skip a day of practice. Not herself a musician, she undertakes a massive research project to learn as much about music as she can, and reproduces in the book some of the voluminous notes she sent her girls critiquing their play. Chua is obsessed with the girls' maximum improvement, and when the girls ask for a dog, and her parents get them one, a Samoyed named Coco, Chua starts in on the dog's education as well. In one of the funnier scenes in the book, Chua berates her husband, also a law professor at Yale, for his lax attitude toward the education of their progeny. "What dreams do you have for Sophia, or for Lulu?" she asks him. "Do you ever even think about that? What are your dreams for Coco?" Her husband laughs. "Dreams for Coco," he says. "That's really funny, Amy."

That scene is, in a way, the book's turning point. Afterward, we see Lulu, Chua's younger daughter, rebel against the violin and take up tennis. And Chua adopts a slightly more laid-back attitude toward the question of her daughters' upbringing.

The book is pretty funny, as I say, though, as is true of a certain kind of writer, you can't always tell when Chua is joking. (A less generous way of putting it is that she says what she really thinks under the cover of jokes, in order later to deny it, if necessary.) But there are two larger, more cosmic jokes in the book that Chua never quite addresses.

One is that while Chua pretends to be a heartless mother who will stop at nothing to see her children achieve greatness, she is in fact, by any measure, a remarkable mother. She spends countless hours with her children, driving them this way and that for music lessons, entering them into competitions, discussing their playing with them. Short of actual abusive parents like John O'Sullivan, who also spent many hours on the road to hockey games with his son, anyone who spends that much time with their kid—whether they're a Chinese mother, a Jewish mother, a Spanish mother; whether they're traveling to music lessons or just to visit grandparents—will be doing a great job. There is nothing specifically Chinese about that.

The other joke is that Amy Chua is not a Chinese immigrant. She was born in the United States. Her father was a math professor at Berkeley. She speaks some Hokkien Chinese, but she sends her kids for Mandarin lessons. (That is, she cannot speak Chinese to her kids!) At one point in the book, Chua encounters actual immigrant parents. They have brought their music-playing children, as she has, to try out for a spot at Juilliard in New York. At first Chua is dismissive. The parents are intense, but their intensity is about a ticket to an elite education, not a proficiency in Bach. "They seem so unsubtle," Chua thinks, "can they possibly love music?" But these criticisms soon give way to a sort of awe. Chua is simply not as fierce and desperate as these people; she is not a true tiger mom. "I don't have what it takes," she says. In the end, her daughter is rejected by the music school but so impresses one of the judges that she is allowed to join her highly sought-after studio, which is almost better.

You can see why people were mad. The book is hyperbolic in its dismissal of "soft" Western parenting styles, but it does advance in earnest the proposition that parents can and should be demanding of their children—that this is not a way of belittling or crushing them, but a statement of belief in their abilities. Chua insists that this is why Chinese families remain closer than Western ones, and you have to read to the end of the book to learn that her own father rejected his family because they wanted him to go into business rather than pursue his passion, which was math. In the end one comes to think that "tiger mom" is a parenting identity that Chua has adopted, having been free to choose from many others, but one that, having chosen it, she plays to the hilt.

And there is one part of the performance of "tiger mom" that feels very real. In a striking passage in the early, hyperbolic part of the book, where Chua presents a scandalous series of ethnographic stereotypes, she describes the generational story of many immigrant families. The initial generation works the hardest, having come in desperation straight off the boat. The next generation, with a memory of that desperation but also with the advantage of cultural proficiency and the financial backing of the initial generation, becomes the most successful. And then the third generation goes to pot. They grow up comfortable, their parents are afraid to yell at them, and eventually they become failures who refuse to move out of the house. Chua calls this phenomenon "generational decline" and wishes at all costs to avoid it. This is the one thing I believe she truly means in the entire book, and that is not contradicted by the book's otherwise softer-hearted second half. Chua and her husband have fought their way to a place in the country's elite, and they have no intention of relinquishing it. Her husband may think that kids should have a happy childhood and question authority— ever the stereotyper, Chua attributes this to his being Jewish— and Chua may think they need to learn to obey, but both agree that they need to keep their class privilege. The tiger mom's lessons turned out not to be about music or perseverance: they were about doing whatever it takes to get ahead and stay there. Readers of the book could have been disappointed, but not truly surprised, when it recently emerged that Sophia, the dutiful older daughter, had taken a clerkship on the Supreme Court with the disgraced justice and political hack Brett Kavanaugh.

MY BIGGEST FLAW AS A PARENT was inconsistency. I wanted to be nice; I wanted to be empathetic; I wanted to be *American*. But I also had inside of me a few unshakable beliefs. I thought Raffi should do his best in school; that he should find something he enjoyed and get good at it; that he should master his immediate environment and become as self-reliant as possible. When I write them out like this, they do not seem like unreasonable beliefs. Unfortunately, in practice, these beliefs were most often expressed in moments of crisis, like when we were taking forever to leave the house, and Emily was trying to jam Raffi's feet into his sneakers, which in fact he was perfectly capable of putting on himself if he felt like it, and so I would yell, much louder than necessary, "He can put on his own sneakers!" Emily did not appreciate this; Raffi did not appreciate this; I knew that no one appreciated it. But I couldn't help it.

I chalked it up to my being Russian. It happened—my yelling, I mean—in Russian, a lot of the time; it reminded me of my own Russian father ("Figure it out yourself"); and it was the opposite of the way Emily, an American, did things. After reading Chua's book, I started thinking about it more. Was there such a thing as *Russian* parenting? If Chua had donned the mantle of the tiger mom, could I don the Russian equivalent? I mentioned it to Emily. "Bear dad," she said immediately. "But you can't call your book that because then people will think it's about being a cute, hairy gay guy."

Bear dad: it was very clever. But was there such a thing? Was my father one? Was I?

It was a little hard to say of what exactly Russian parenting consisted. There was so much upheaval in Russia in the twentieth century—so many parents arrested, their property expropriated; so many families exiled. A common experience in my parents' generation was the absence of fathers entirely: millions of them had perished during the war, my mother's father among them. In a famous scene in Marlen Khutsiev's 1962 film *Zastava Ilyicha (Ilyich's Gate)*, about the situation of Soviet youth in the early 1960s, the aimless young protagonist dreams that he meets his father, who died in the war. He wants his father's advice on what to do with his life. His father answers with a question: "How old are you?" The answer is twenty-three. "And I'm twenty-one," says the father. "How can I give you advice?"

Even after the war generation passed and there were more men around, still they remained largely absent. They drank too much or wandered off. In Moscow, I had three aunts. Two were single mothers and the third eventually divorced her husband, remarried, and moved to Israel. People got married too young, had too little money, and often had to live with their parents. Masha and I were the only ones among the cousins who grew up with the same two parents.

There were some books written for Soviet parents, and of course a great deal of state ideology. Anton Makarenko, a kind of Soviet John Dewey, was hugely influential in the rhetoric and some of the practices of Soviet educational institutions, but his work did not really address or penetrate the realm of family life. For a while Chukovsky, the great children's poet, was looked to as an authority on child-rearing. But I happened to know that my Western-oriented parents, when raising me, mostly read the advice of Dr. Spock, whose *Baby and Child Care* was first published in the USSR in a Russian translation in 1970, just a few years before my birth.

I tried to interview my Russian relatives about Russian parenting. My father, as usual, refused to generalize; he could address specific situations, but he didn't have a theory of parenting. My aunt Lenna emphasized that we were not Russians, but Jews; Jewish parenting, she said, was an entirely separate endeavor, marked by overprotection and love. My sibling, Masha, who now lived in New York after being hounded out of Russia, said the chief distinguishing characteristic of Russian parenting was a hatred of children. They started texting me observations from around the city. From a park in Brooklyn one morning: "Saw a guy who was looking at his kid like he hated her, and I thought, Russian. Sure enough, when I got closer: 'Вставай! Иди! Кому говорю.'" That is: "Get up! Let's go! I'm talking to you." It's how one would address a lazy dog.

A short while after Raffi turned four, he and I spent a week in the former Soviet republic of Georgia in the company of my aunt Sveta, who lives in Moscow. It's the closest we've come, at this point, to Russia, and we had, mostly, a good time. We climbed around a prehistoric cave city, attended some fervent anti-Russian protests (PUTIN, SUCK MY DICK was one Russian-language poster I did not read aloud to Raffi), and visited the Stalin Museum in Gori, an unreconstructed monument to Georgia's most famous native son. (Raffi was delighted and fascinated by this exposure to a real-live bad guy, the sort of person he'd been reading about in his superhero books but had never encountered outside them.) We stayed in a tiny two-bedroom Airbnb, and the entire time I was terrified of what Aunt Sveta would make of my parenting. She had raised my cousin Mitya on her own after her hard-drinking ex-husband left for another woman (he is famous in our family for infuriating my aunt Lenna when, while staying briefly at her place when she was out of town, he managed to drink not only her perfume, which she didn't care about, but also a very nice bottle of Armenian cognac, which she was saving for a special occasion). In our family, Aunt Sveta is a person of considerable moral stature and a perceptive critic of family dysfunction. I was worried that she would think me too strict a parent, too much of a yeller. Instead, toward the end of the week—a week during which Raffi was mostly a good sport but also went to bed every night at two A.M., because of the time difference, and also delightedly trampled on some nice plants at a fancy outdoor Georgian restaurant, and hit an older boy he'd met in the face with a stick—Aunt Sveta said something like the opposite. She thought I catered too much to Raffi's every whim and organized my entire existence around him. "Someday someone is going to tell him no," she said, "and he won't know what to do." To Emily, I seemed too strict; to Aunt Sveta, a total pushover.

In the course of these reflections on Russian parenting, I arranged a call with Natalia Kandror, my childhood pediatrician in Boston. Kandror had been for some time the only Russian pediatrician in the Boston area, and I thought that, as a Russian doctor seeing both Russian and American patients in an American context, she might have a panoptic view of the differences between them.

Dr. Kandror told me a bit of her story. She had finished medical school in Moscow in 1961 and done a three-year tour in the pediatric unit at a hospital north of the Arctic Circle. Her patients were the children of Arctic shipping workers, airport staff, and those who had been released from the labor camps in the 1950s but couldn't yet return to the big cities. In 1980, she immigrated to the U.S. Like all foreign doctors, she had to take two main exams before starting to practice: one for medical knowledge, administered by the National Board of Medical

Examiners, and another, the TOEFL, for English. She studied hard for the medical exam and passed, but she didn't get a high enough score on the TOEFL the first three times she took it. After that, she stopped waiting for the results; she would take the test and immediately sign up for the next one. In the end she took the TOEFL six times, and received a passing score on the last three.

She started a residency at Boston City Hospital and found it immensely difficult. She had been a working doctor for two decades, but medicine was practiced differently in the U.S. It was more technical, based more on statistics; it deployed many more resources for each patient; and the practitioners were better educated. "A nurse in America knew more than a medical school graduate in the Soviet Union," she told me. For six months, Kandror felt like she was in over her head. She couldn't understand much of what was said, and even when her technical vocabulary improved, she found she didn't know how to speak to patients, how to say "Turn your head" or "Look up." Finally, though, her experience kicked in. Her English improved. She finished the residency and then started working as a pediatrician. She was immensely popular and revered. Masha and I both came to see her, and years later, when Masha was living in Moscow, they would take their kids to see Kandror whenever they visited my father during the summer.

I asked for Dr. Kandror's impressions of Russian versus American parenting. She answered immediately. It seemed like she'd given it a lot of thought.

Russian parents, she said, were constantly criticizing their children. "They would sit in my waiting room and in that short time they would make fifteen or twenty criticisms of their child," she said. "American parents would sit there for the same amount of time and make zero." The American way, she thought, was clearly preferable.

Russians were also not very good at keeping up with the way their children changed over time. "A child who is ten or twelve or thirteen, you have to understand that he is his own person, or on his way to becoming his own person," she said. "You can't treat him the way you did when he was five." Russians tended to want their kids to stay in line, and this often backfired. It led to a loss of trust between child and parent. Americans were better at giving their kids some space, she said.

I was not surprised to hear this. There were many things that Russians of my parents' generation disliked about America, but overall they thought it was a wonderful place. They had come here of their own free will and most of them never regretted it. They criticized Americans in a pro forma way; their real zeal was in criticizing their countrymen. Still, I asked Kandror if there were things about Russian child-rearing that she admired, that we should keep. Somewhat reluctantly, she said yes. She liked that Russian children were taught manners; she was horrified by American children who were permitted to say "shut up" to their parents. She liked the Russian tradition of teaching children to memorize short poems. And she liked the Russian emphasis on academics.

I said that Americans—by which I meant a particular type of white, liberal, middle-class American, like Emily—tended to downplay academics.

"I think that's a mistake," said Kandror. "We both know that it opens up the world to you and makes life easier later on."

We did. I did. I did know that.

But how, I said, do you take the good from the Russian method without taking the bad? It seemed like something that was hard to do halfway. Take my case. I wasn't criticizing Raffi twenty times in twenty minutes, but maybe ten times, or maybe five. And the result was neither this nor that, and possibly even the worst of both worlds. I got the bad parts of the Russian method—Raffi's resentment, his distrust, his fear—without really any of the good: his discipline, his good manners. He had, as a matter of fact, started saying "shut up" to us. And my disagreements with Emily on the subject of discipline were the worst thing of all: on that, at least, everyone could agree.

Dr. Kandror didn't have an answer to that. She told me about a Russian family she knew who had tried to raise their daughter in the American way. As a result, she had had trouble at school and dropped out. Now, in her twenties, she couldn't really get on her feet. Her parents, said Dr. Kandror, did not want their daughter to be afraid of them, and she isn't. "Instead, she's afraid of everything else."

I added this to my list of parental tragedies and disappointments. There were so many of them. There is no tragedy like the tragedy of parenthood. And there was no answer, no perfect formula of Russian and American parenting, that was going to magically make it go away.

EVERYONE I GREW UP WITH, the Americanized children of Russian immigrant parents in the Boston area, turned out OK. Eugene Alperovich became a doctor, Motya Yankelevich got a PhD in literature and became a publisher, Masha Rapoport became an artist and writer. I also became a writer. It was a nice thing in our community that writers were admired. It was some combination of the Russian literary tradition, the logocentrism of the Soviet regime, and the fact that so much resistance to the regime came from writers. Many young émigré Russians went into literature, as well as medicine and computers.

We all did fine, I think, are doing fine. But if you look a little deeper, it becomes more complex. There was such an emphasis on achievement—on doing all the things that our parents, because they were Jews and because they grew up in a devastated country, under Communism, could not do—that it couldn't help but warp us a little. Some of us did not get married or have kids, or if we did, we did so later. There was no cult of domesticity where we came from—100 percent of our mothers worked outside the home, as computer programmers or doctors or literary critics, and 0 percent of them took pride in their cooking. My mom used to fry a pork chop and heat some peas out of a can, and we would all sit at the table and scarf it down while we read our books. I still like to read while eating: it strikes me as the highest form of leisure. So, anyway, though most of us came from stable families, reproducing those families was not anyone's priority. The whole idea was to do what our parents had not been able to.

Some years ago, when I was living with my grandmother in Moscow, I found a packet of letters that my mother had written to her after we moved to the States. My mother was my grandmother's only child, and they were very close; for the first two years the letters were incredibly frequent, as many as two per week. They described in minute detail our acclimation to the States, my mother's social circle, my father's first job offer. My mother, mostly, was pleased with what she and my father had done. But occasionally you could catch a glimpse of her sadness and loneliness. In one of the letters she talked about seven-year-old me asking her why we had left the USSR. "After all, we had an apartment, and we weren't starving, and we had money," I apparently said. My mom was bereft. "When I tried to explain it to him," she wrote to my grandmother, "at his level, he said, 'What, are we just going to live like this without relatives our whole lives?' I said that you would all come here eventually, or we would come to visit you. To which he answered quite reasonably that Baba Seva"—my great-grandmother, who was by then in her nineties—"wasn't ever going to come. My heart just sank. How does he understand all this, at his age? And the thing is, it'll never be possible to explain it to him. That is, we'll be able to explain it, but he won't understand any of it, because he won't ever have known anything other than this comfort and ease (at least, so I hope)."

I wonder what I might have been thinking as I gave my mother a hard time. Did I really miss my relatives so much? Was I—more likely—just repeating back to her something that I thought *she* felt? I have no memory of it. I certainly have no memory of pining for the USSR. But who knows. Anyway, what my mom could not have known at the time was that the Soviet Union would soon fall apart, and I would have a chance to see, at least in some form, the lives they used to have, and understand much better why they left them. But that was later, and by the time it happened my mom was gone.

We did grow up comfortable, American, but also confused about where we'd come from, and how exactly we were supposed to feel about it. My parents and their friends never spent a minute wondering about their "identity." It wasn't because they were simple people to whom a metaphysical concept like identity was out of reach. It was because they knew exactly who they were—they were educated Russian Jews who had emigrated to America. Some of us had come from Moscow and some had come from Leningrad. That was a difference worth thinking about. Anything more general did not apply.

But who were we, their children? And who were *our* children? When Raffi was in pre-K, he was asked to decorate a paper doll with his "culture." This was a way of teaching diversity to the kids. Your classmates were Black and Indian and Jewish, and it was OK! But what was Raffi's culture? Was he

Russian? Jewish? Part WASP? (Emily is part WASP, on her mother's side.) I don't know if other families in our class, in particular the many cross-cultural families, had as much trouble with the culture doll as we did. Probably not. But it seemed to me like all of us were pretty far away from wherever our parents, or their parents, had started.

In the end, the night before it was due, we stapled some pictures of Emily's parents onto the doll and added some elements of a Soviet Red Army uniform. In those months Raffi had become interested in the subject of war, and I explained to him that his great-grandfather had died fighting the Nazis. This was a year after Charlottesville, and I felt like it was OK for Raffi to know that his ancestors had once fought Nazis. But the whole thing felt a little fake. Raffi was not fighting Nazis! He didn't even like borscht.

A YEAR AFTER TIGER MOM unsettled American parents who wondered if their children were going to be displaced by Chinese superachievers, yet another book dropped on the American market with a message about superior parenting somewhere else: in France. Pamela Druckerman's *Bringing Up Bébé* (or, in the UK, *French Children Don't Throw Food*) soon found itself on the bestseller list. It is a perfect storm of anxiety-producing advice, designed to make its American readers feel harried, disheveled, and fat, but offering tips (helpfully enumerated in Druckerman's follow-up, *Bébé Day by Day: 100 Keys to French Parenting*) on how to avoid this fate.

The book is *incroyable*. It starts with an account of Druckerman (a former *Wall Street Journal* reporter) and her husband (a British-born soccer writer for the *Financial Times*) taking their toddler out to eat at a French resort. The toddler behaves like a toddler, throws things onto the floor, refuses to eat anything interesting. Looking around, embarrassed, Druckerman sees that there are French toddlers at the restaurant who are behaving quite reasonably, sitting quietly and patiently, and eating all sorts of cheeses. How do the French do it? she wonders. And so Druckerman launches an investigation into French parenting.

She learns that French parents are stricter than American ones; that they enforce mealtimes, bedtimes, and a modicum of polite behavior (there is an entire chapter on how French parents force their children to say *bonjour* to adults). The great discovery in the book is what Druckerman calls *"le pause"*—the brief delay that French parents take before picking up their infants when the infants are crying. After all, the infants may just be clearing their throats, or rolling over; they aren't necessarily having a crisis that needs to be addressed. Druckerman finds that the French employ *le pause* uniformly, as a matter of course, and that it is the key to having infants sleeping through the night at a very early age. Our very own Michel Cohen, author of my favorite baby advice book, makes a cameo appearance as an emissary of the French parenting tradition in New York.

Druckerman also finds that the French have free, high-quality day cares (known as crèches, from the old German for "crib," also, in English, used to refer to the scene of the Nativity); that French grandparents tend to live within driving or walking distance of children and are willing to take them for weeks at a time; and of course that French women, even when they are pregnant, do not get fat.

Some of what Druckerman describes is very appealing. Who doesn't want their little babies to sleep peacefully through the night without the torture of cry-it-out? Who doesn't want their children to eat calmly and sample a variety of cheeses? Who doesn't want their children to say *bonjour*?

But all this comes at a cost, a very high cost, and while I wouldn't say that Druckerman conceals it, she does bury it a little. You have to read to the midpoint of the book before you learn that French women hardly breastfeed. They associate it with the peasantry and believe that it's bad for the shape of your breasts. Druckerman has some incisive things to say about the American obsession with breastfeeding, which she likens to a mothering competition, and which really isn't based on science: The WHO recommends that women breastfeed children until the age of two, but that's only because many women in the developing world don't have access to clean water with which to mix their formula. Otherwise, formula is fine. But still, when I read about French women's attitudes toward breastfeeding, I laughed. *Of course* French children sleep through the night earlier, develop more independence (earlier), and start trying new foods—their mothers aren't feeding them to sleep at night, aren't comforting them with the breast when they're scared. And that is fine. But it seems to have a great deal more explanatory power for why French kids sleep at night than *le pause*, and, more important, it is almost certainly not something that most of Druckerman's readers would choose to do. Druckerman herself, she admits, breastfed her children much longer than a French mother would.

For all its flaws, the book is extremely well done and has been incredibly influential. It spawned an entire series of books about superior parenting styles in other cultures: *The Happiest Kids in the World* (Dutch parenting, 2016); *The Danish Way of Parenting* (2017); *There's No Such Thing as Bad Weather* (Swedish parenting, 2017); *Achtung Baby* (German parenting, 2018). None of these books is as sharp or as interesting as Druckerman's, and Druckerman for her part seems to be having second thoughts about the mini-genre she has created. In a recent *New York Times* review of the latest entrant—*Hunt, Gather, Parent: What Ancient Cultures Can Teach Us About the Lost Art of Raising Happy, Helpful Little Humans*—Druckerman refers to "the now extensive literature, mostly written for Americans by Americans, about the sensible, calmer ways that people in other countries raise kids. (I'm guilty of adding to the pile.)" This parenthetical is, assuredly, not giving herself enough credit.

Emily read *Bringing Up Bébé* before Raffi was born; it was

one of many books she read in preparation, but still she urged us, when Raffi was little, to employ *le pause*. It didn't work. Raffi would just keep crying, and we would fetch him. Druckerman was right about American parenting—it made us crazy and miserable. She was wrong about the solution—we were not going to become French parents. But I, like tiger mom, had access to a different tradition. I could still become bear dad, if I really tried.

THE BOOK THAT CURED me of this nonsense—that cured me of a lot of nonsense—was written by a professor of developmental psychology named Jonathan Tudge. It came out in 2008 and is called *The Everyday Lives of Young Children: Culture, Class, and Child Rearing in Diverse Societies*. It describes a large study, designed by Tudge, of small children's everyday activities in seven countries: Russia, Estonia, Finland, Kenya, South Korea, Brazil, and the U.S. Tudge makes a point in each place of studying the children of both middle-class and working-class parents. Part of the idea is to try to compare like to like—in many cross-cultural studies, Tudge writes, a middle-class (almost always white) American family would be compared to a rural family from, say, Kenya. (That was the case in that *Babies* documentary we watched.) Such studies certainly captured some of the interesting differences between child-rearing approaches across different places, but they were also in their way misleading. In fact, writes Tudge, a middle-class family in Kenya is not that different from a middle-class family in the U.S., though the differences that do exist can still be of interest.

For his study, Tudge sent out a team of grad students to gather data on what three-year-olds actually did with their time in these various places. The results are interesting and at times surprising. Kids in America watched more TV than kids in other places (except South Korea), and in almost all places (except Estonia) greater TV watching correlated with less conversation, fewer lessons, and less play. Kids in Finland engaged in significantly more conversation than anyone else. The reason for this was mysterious. Kids in Estonia and Russia tended to receive more "lessons," primarily in the form of physical processes being explained to them by parents and grandparents. This one could be explained. It was not that Russians and Estonians were more academically minded than other parents, but that their economies had cratered after the Soviet collapse, and many of them took to cultivating small gardens to help supplement their food supply. As a result, they had numerous opportunities to explain to their children and grandchildren how plants grew, what water and sunlight were for, and how to protect vegetables from wind and frost. For the same reason, and with similar results, Russians and Estonians also tended to fix more of their electronics, rather than throwing them away, again giving them opportunities to explain the world to their children.

Tudge manages to be magnificently nonjudgmental about all this. He does not recoil in horror at the TV-watching habits of the Americans, nor scream with delight at the talkativeness of the Finns. He is, as he explains, a "contextualist," in the tradition of Lev Vygotsky, Urie Bronfenbrenner, and Barbara Rogoff, and not just a contextualist but a "cultural-ecological" one. He does not believe in some kind of normative or ideal form of child development. Rather, children grow up in the culture in which they grow up, which values certain things and does things a certain way. Pushing back against his mentor Bronfenbrenner's idea that a proper education will take the form of increasingly complex interactions (or "proximal processes," as Bronfenbrenner calls them) between parent and child, Tudge writes that development "will occur even if a parent continues to behave in the same manner toward the child or in a progressively less complex fashion. What matters for development is the way in which people typically act and interact with objects, symbols, and the social world, without any regard for the apparent appropriateness of that development." And, further on: "Cultural groups with values, beliefs, lifestyles, and patterns of social interchange different from those found in North American middle-class communities [will] necessarily value different types of proximal processes. . . . What counts as more complex to one group might be viewed as less complex by another."

I admit I was stunned by these passages. I felt rebuked by them. All the time I'd spent worrying over whether Raffi was being sufficiently enriched by our parenting; whether teaching him Russian was good for him or watching TV was bad for him; whether he should sleep in his socks (no). It didn't matter.

Development, writes Tudge, will occur even if the parent . . . does nothing. Or at least doesn't do anything in particular. Development will occur!

While reading Tudge's book, I couldn't quite rid myself of the habit of reading as a consumer. I wanted Raffi to talk as much as a Finn, learn as much about the world from his parents as a Russian or Estonian, and become as practiced in the ways of empathy and nurturance as a boy from the Luo tribe in Kenya who was tasked with the traditionally female care of the family baby because there were not enough girls around. A 1973 study of the Luo by the anthropologist Carol Ember, cited by Tudge, found that in these circumstances boys as young as five became more nurturing: they exhibited "less overall egoism, more pro-social behavior, less egoistic aggression, and less egoistic dependency" compared with boys who were allowed to skip these tasks. That sounded good to me. A little of this and a little of that, I thought as I read, and you could create the perfect kid.

But Tudge's whole point is that you cannot simply pick and choose. These skills, these competencies, are developed in very specific cultural and historical circumstances, for particular reasons. If I did not garden to survive, Raffi was not going to learn about vegetables. If we hired a babysitter for Ilya, Raffi was not going to become a nurturer. And in fact even the Luo were changing—as their rural economy died out, as literacy became more prized as an engine of economic mobility, they were forced to send their kids to school and hire babysitters, just like everyone else.

Raffi and Emily and I were stuck in our concrete cultural and historical circumstances. We could reject some of these and adopt some others. In Tudge's study, too, there were Finnish kids who did not talk a lot and American kids who did not watch TV. We had some agency. But we were where we were; we could not pretend we were members of the Luo tribe, or post-Soviet Estonians living in the ruins of the once mighty empire.

Tudge's book was accessibly written but it was published by Cambridge University Press for an academic audience. Certain of his conclusions were implicit; in places he was in dialogue with authors I hadn't read. In short, I wanted to ask some follow-up questions. He agreed to chat over Skype.

We had just moved—again—back to our old neighborhood. We were closer to Raffi's school and Ilya's preschool. If there was one thing that we had learned as parents, one inviolable rule, it was that you should be as close as possible to your kids' day cares. This is the secret to happiness. I share it now with you.

I sat in our new apartment, surrounded by boxes, and talked with Tudge. He turned out to be a genial Jewish Englishman in late middle age who now split his time between the United States and southern Brazil, where his second wife, also a developmental psychologist and researcher, lived. We discussed his book. He teased out a problem with the theory of cultural-ecological contextualism that I had not quite understood, which was the problem of relativism. It was one thing, and pretty un-controversial in most circles, to say that the parenting strategies of Finns were no better than those of South Koreans, which were no better than those of Brazilians, because in the context of their own societies, they did what was necessary to succeed. But when faced with two cultural groups existing in the *same* society, said Tudge, "you've got a real problem. We can say, until we're blue in the face, that this cultural group has these sets of values that are different from this other cultural group that has these other sets of values. You and I would say it's im-possible to say which is better outside of the terms of the cul-tural group itself. But both of these groups are within this society." They are competing for the same limited set of re-sources. And one *can* say, for a given society, which set of prac-tices is going to lead to better outcomes.

On the other hand, said Tudge, one could argue or even insist that those societal values or practices needed to change, which was another way of saying that society needed to change.

I decided that if anyone could answer my question about the right way to parent, it was Tudge. I went ahead and asked him what I should do, what sort of parent I should be.

Here, Tudge was less certain. "Be true to yourself," he sug-gested.

But what is the self?

Tudge acknowledged that the self was malleable.

I told him that Emily and I fought a lot about how to raise

Raffi, and that I felt these fights reflected our differing cultural backgrounds.

He pushed back. He said that this was nothing new, that in his experience parents from identical cultural backgrounds also often had fights about child-rearing. "Cultural groups are not homogeneous," he said. "You can be from the same cultural group and have *tons* of arguments about how kids should be raised."

What then, I asked?

Tudge finally admitted that there wasn't much anyone could do. He used his own experience as an example. He had devoted his life to studying the development of young people all over the world, in comparative perspective; then he became a father. "It didn't really matter how much I read or how much I thought about how one brings up a child," he told me. "I realized when I was bringing up mine that I was treating her like my dad treated me. And it wasn't very good. I wasn't happy with the way I was raised!"

But he couldn't help it. None of us can.

A FEW DAYS AFTER I spoke with Tudge, I took Raffi and Ilya to the playground. It was a Sunday, our house was still filled with boxes, and I wanted to get the boys out of Emily's hair for a few hours. In order to get them excited about going, I allowed them each to choose their mode of conveyance. This turned out to be a mistake. Ilya, just a little older than two, chose his scooter,

and Raffi, five years and change, chose his bike (still with training wheels on). Neither of them was competent at riding these
vehicles, but I said yes.

Ilya scooted for a block and then started falling off his
scooter. I didn't see the first time he fell, just that he was lying
on the ground, and I picked him up. Then it happened again.
"Those are fake falls, Dada!" Raffi called out to me. "He's only
pretending to fall."

I was confused by this information, but it turned out to be
true. Ilya would scoot for a bit and then throw himself to the
ground. I wasn't sure why. I would wait for a little while—*le
pause*—and then when he remained on the ground, I would pick
him up again. This annoyed Raffi to no end, since he didn't feel
Ilya deserved to get picked up, since he had, after all, deliberately fallen down. "That is fake falling!" Raffi kept saying. But
Raffi was having his own problems, since our way to the playground was ever so slightly uphill and he hadn't yet figured out
how to ride uphill on his crazy-looking bike that my father had
gotten him at Walmart. He would get stuck about once a block
and huff and puff, and eventually I would have to give him a
push to get him going again. When he started in on Ilya about
fake falling, I didn't have much patience for it. "Work on yourself!" I told him. "Don't worry about Ilya." When, at one point,
Ilya had fallen and been picked up again, Raffi rode over to him
and grabbed his face and shoved him. I hated that. "*Ostav' ego
v pokoe!*" I yelled. Leave him alone!

Three blocks into our journey, Raffi got stuck again and I was too far ahead, pulling Ilya's scooter, to help. A young couple with a baby was walking in the same direction, and the mom gave Raffi a push. Then another one. I felt embarrassed—as if I had taken on more than I could handle, which I had—and maybe Raffi did as well. When he yelled again that Ilya was a faker, I told him to concentrate on learning to ride his bike. "Dada!" he yelled back. "You are making everyone think that I've never ridden a bike before!"

"That's not true!" I said. "Anyway, no one understands Russian."

Finally, we turned a corner and reached level ground. Raffi rode more easily now. Ilya had stopped deliberately falling off his scooter, but now he kept getting off to study the beautiful wrought-iron fences along this stretch of street. During one such stop, Raffi sped up on his bike and plowed directly into Ilya. Ilya went flying.

Angrily I pulled Raffi off his bike and then picked up the crying Ilya. I turned to Raffi and started yelling. "What are you doing?" I said.

"I didn't know that was going to happen," Raffi said, which was something he had taken to saying whenever he hit Ilya or tripped him up, as if he were just experimentally sticking out his fist or his foot.

"You didn't know if you went directly at him, you would hit him?"

He didn't answer. I wasn't even very mad—a little shocked,

maybe, but once I saw Ilya was OK, not furious—but I felt I couldn't ignore what Raffi had done.

"Let's take a break from the bike for a little while," I said, and we walked the rest of the way to the playground, me carrying Ilya and his scooter with one hand and walking Raffi's bike with the other. When we got to the next intersection, I put Ilya down. Raffi held his hand as we crossed the street.

"Dada," he said, "if people understood Russian, they would say, 'That guy is not nice.'"

"I'm nice," I said. "But what did you think I would do when you hit Ilya?"

"When you yell like that, I get sad and I get scared."

"I don't want to scare you," I said. "I never want to scare you. But you can't hit Ilya."

"You don't love me."

"I love you. I love you very, very much."

"Then why do you yell at me?"

"Listen, my dad used to yell at me. And he yelled at Masha and Daniel and Philip. And Mama and I yell at each other all the time."

"Grown-ups don't count."

We kept walking. I was still a little mad at him, but also impressed by how articulate he was being, how he had managed to locate the source of his sadness and begun to talk about it. He hadn't learned that from me, but he had learned it.

He said, "Dada, you are a liar. Every time you say you won't get mad, and then you get mad again."

This was true. I did promise that, and then I always broke that promise. But now I said, "I will always get mad when you hit Ilya! I never promised not to yell at you if you did that. The opposite: I will definitely yell at you when you do that."

At this point we had arrived at the playground. Raffi was tired of arguing with me and ran right in. There was no one there that he knew, and he ended up spending a lot of time playing with his brother. For the most part, he managed to play nicely: he could be very gentle and loving when he wanted to be.

As for me I thought again about my anger. I still yelled at Raffi much more than I would have liked, then felt bad about it. A few weeks earlier, not long after another blowup, we had been in the park with Raffi's old preschool friend A. Raffi and A. played a game in which they pretended their parents were gone and they were assigned new parents. I asked Raffi what his pretend parents were like, and he said, "Nice and gentle." I felt caught out by this. Those were words that didn't describe me very well. If I was a bear dad, I was a reluctant or unconscious one.

While I was pondering all this at the playground, a little girl a year or two older than Raffi threw a terrible tantrum—she was trying to do the rings, i.e., swing on the jungle gym rings from one to the next, and was almost managing to do them, very impressively, but she couldn't quite get it. Her father was encouraging and kind, but she didn't hear him. She became increasingly frustrated, and when her father said it was time to go home for dinner, she refused. It took them half an hour to leave.

The entire time I thought that the father was doing a remarkable job of staying calm, of not yelling, of not asserting his authority. I envied his patience. But I could not do what he was doing—and, I suddenly realized, in a kind of Tudgean epiphany, *I would not want to.* It wasn't in me. When it's time to leave the playground, you need to leave the fucking playground.

As for us, we were not in a hurry and we stayed until it got dark. Raffi said he wanted to be the last person there, and we almost were. Finally, without any problem, we left. On the way home, the slight slope of the hill was in our favor. Raffi rode his bike well, and when things were uphill or too hectic, he got off and walked with it.

We made it home and the kids had dinner. Then, while they watched a movie, Emily and I had dinner. Ilya went to bed easily—at nine—but Raffi was in a bit of a mood and stayed up almost until ten. I did the last bit of reading with him in his new bed. Emily had been reading the Moomintroll books to him, and I read to him about the Hemulen who shows up at the Moomintroll residence and tries to get everyone to ski. There follows a socially complicated situation in which all the other guests get tired of the Hemulen and want him to leave but don't quite know how to say so. These were books that I remembered my mother reading to me, in Russian, right around this age. Raffi listened attentively and then finally fell asleep.

"What an angel," I said to Emily, as I always do once Raffi is asleep.

"A beautiful angel," she agreed.

We lay down exhausted in our bed. There were still stray boxes of stuff and books that we hadn't yet unpacked, but while I'd been at the playground with the kids, Emily had put most of the boxes in various closets and, crucially, put the rug down in the living room. Our apartment looked like a home. Our family looked like a family. I was from Russia and yelled. Emily was from Maryland and was calm and empathetic. Raffi would probably be in our bed, kicking us, in a matter of hours. It was time to go to sleep.

Epilogue: Raffi at Six

Raffi at six can brush his own teeth and floss and use mouthwash. He can pick out clothes and dress himself without complaint. He can tie his own shoelaces. He can read and write, though his spelling is a work in progress. When going to a birthday party for one of his friends, he is, most of the time, willing to sit down and make a card. He almost always writes the same thing: "I love you. You are the best. Frum Raffi."

He is still relentlessly himself. He is energetic and demanding; quick to take offense and quick to forgive. He is no longer that hard to put to sleep—pretty much no matter what, he conks out between 9 and 9:30 P.M.—but he still gets up too early. Once up, he drags a chair into the kitchen, puts Ilya's little step stool on top of it, and raids the upper kitchen cabinets in search of candy.

When I started writing these essays, I thought this was just what kids were like. One of my impulses was to reach out to other parents and ask: Are you seeing this too? Do your kids do this? And the answer, in a lot of cases, was yes. It turns out a lot of little kids are total maniacs. Left to their own devices, they would definitely murder themselves and one another.

But the answer was also no. There were things that Raffi had entered into the annals of child behavior with no precedent in human history. This was true of other kids as well. They invented ways to destroy their homes, or torture their parents or siblings, that no one had thought of before. This is how humanity advances.

The thing I didn't expect was Raffi's *consistency*, his integrity. As he was at three months, so he was at three years, and so he is now at six. He's different, to be sure: He can walk and talk and even reason with us. He has an understanding of the future and the past, though he still refers to the days of the week as "the first day" (Monday), "the second day" (Tuesday), etc., until we get to the weekend, at which point it becomes "the first weekend day," then the second. He is perpetually disappointed that there isn't a third. But it's still Raffi in there, ever changing but the same.

THE FRENCH NOVELIST Michel Houellebecq has an essay on parenthood in which he talks about how he likes his son well enough, except for those traits of his that resemble the boy's mother's. What he really wants, Houellebecq realizes, is a clone.

It's a keen insight. But I wonder, when I look at my conflicts with Raffi, whether the worst of them are over traits or habits that are his mother's, so that in a way I am continuing my arguments with her through him, or whether they are over the traits and habits that I dislike most in myself. Emily says that it's funny to watch Raffi and me fight because we look so much alike. "It's like watching a person arguing with himself in the mirror." On the other hand, Raffi himself recently said to Emily during school drop-off—the moment in the day when he is at his sweetest and most contemplative—that, though he looks like Dada on the outside, on the inside he is more like her. I don't know who's right. When I look at him, at how beautiful he is, it is clear to me that it is Emily's beauty that has found its expression there, not mine. But increasingly I find myself seeing in him a person completely separate from both of us. This is obvious, I suppose, but I never cease to be surprised by it. How did that happen? I don't know; it just did.

I told him recently that I was writing this book and that it would be called *Raising Raffi*. He asked, reasonably enough, why it wasn't also about Ilya. I said that it was called that because with him, with Raffi, we had experienced everything for the first time. I said, "You know how Ilya hits us sometimes?"

"Yes," said Raffi.

"Well, now we know that's just what three-year-olds do. But when you were doing it, we didn't know that."

"And you yelled at me?" said Raffi.

"Yes," I said.

"That's not fair!" said Raffi.

I agreed that it wasn't fair.

RAFFI'S RUSSIAN COMPREHENSION CONTINUES to be good; his speaking continues to be pretty much nonexistent, though once in a while he'll agree to repeat a Russian phrase if I say it first. The other day he asked me when I had first started speaking Russian to him, and said I should have pretended not to know English, so that his Russian could have developed better. We were hoping to go to Russia in the summer of 2020, but COVID interfered. And we were hoping to go this summer, summer of 2022, but then Russia invaded Ukraine. We are not going to Russia this summer.

Raffi is doing well in first grade. The school is still very strict—there is a behavior chart on the wall of his classroom, running from "superstar student" to "call home"—but he seems willing to play along. Sometimes he comes home with a lot of pent-up energy and chases his brother around the apartment, claiming that he was a "star student all day" and now needs to get his crazies out. But most of the time he comes home exhausted from sitting and running and playing all day, and occasionally tells a story about a classmate who said a bad word in the bathroom or did something inappropriate during recess. He has made a lot of good friends at school. "I am," he recently told me, by virtue of all the time he spends there, "a well-known person at my school."

Raffi's hockey playing has slowed. The class we took during

the pandemic winter did not delight him, and this year he refused to sign up again. I've decided to respect that decision, for now. On the other hand, a few months ago, at his insistence, we took the training wheels off his bike and went to the nearest playground. Almost right away, Raffi was able to pedal and accelerate and stay on the bike. What it turned out he couldn't do was stop. He kept crashing into the fence at the edge of the playground. But he didn't give up. By the time we left the playground, Raffi could ride a bike.

He still says "maskes" (and "ghostes"). But he can get his brother dressed and also motivate him. "Yaya," he says, because when Ilya was a toddler he called himself Yaya, "if you get dressed you can have some ice cream!" He spends a lot of time harassing and grabbing things from Ilya, but can also cheer him up when he is sad and crying. "Yaya, here is your robot. You can play with him." Raffi gives him one of his robots. "Look, Yaya, your panda wants to play with him."

"He's too little," says Ilya of his panda.

"No, he's not! Look, he's playing."

He is adorable, infuriating, mercurial. He has finally stopped coming into our bed in the middle of the night. This is a very good thing, because he is now so big, and also because Ilya has started doing it.

He still treats us like servants. While watching TV on a recent evening: "Dada, can I have dessert? I asked you two times already."

He is still unlike anyone we've ever met.

Acknowledgments

I am incredibly grateful to the editors who supported this book as it was being written: Carla Blumenkranz; Molly Fischer; Nikil Saval; Sheila Glaser. Of course this would not have become an actual book without Allison Lorentzen at Viking, also the editor of *A Terrible Country*.

A number of people read this book in different stages of disarray and gave invaluable feedback: Emily Gould, A. J. Brown, Rebecca Curtis, Eric Rosenblum, Chad Harbach, Masha Gessen, Mark Greif. I am very lucky to know such brilliant people.

Ruth Curry offered a spare room in her apartment during the darkest days of the lockdown; Rebecca and Jeremy Glick gave me a place to stay and moral support while I was going through the last draft. Alexander Gessen opened the doors of the Gessen Writing Retreat to me.

I'm grateful to my colleagues at the Columbia Journalism School for their generous and thoughtful feedback and forbearance throughout this project. I benefited greatly from conversations about the project with Michael Shapiro and Nick Lemann.

ACKNOWLEDGMENTS

Sarah Chalfant and Rebecca Nagel at the Wylie Agency were advocates for the book when I wasn't sure it could exist.

I'm very grateful to the team at Viking who has shepherded this book to publication: Camille Leblanc, Ryan Boyle, Jane Cavolina, Sara Delozier.

It would take too long and possibly cause embarrassment if I listed all the parents who've given me useful advice and guidance over the years, but I would be remiss not to mention Eric Rosenblum, Rachael Rosenblum, Emma Jaster, Matt Pearson, Rebecca Winkel, Stephanie Rabins, Michael Haggerty, Sarah Berger, Roy Goodman, Tommy White, Ohad Meroni, Hannah Gladstein, Brandon Buskey, Kate Marvel, Mark Rosin, Gideon Lewis-Kraus, Carol Cohen, George Sirignano, Eddie Joyce, Loren McArthur, Michael Woodsworth, Ben McGrath, Nick Paumgarten, Daniel Alarcón, Duy Linh Tu, Svetlana Solodovnik.

I'm grateful to Raffi and Ilya for allowing themselves to be put under the care of babysitters and teachers and their mother so I could work on this book. I'm grateful to Kate and Rob Gould for Camp Grandma, and for so much else.

Above all, I'm grateful to Emily—my wife, Raffi and Ilya's mother—without whom there would be nothing at all. This book is dedicated to her.